UNIVERSITY
LIBRARIES

VIRES ARTES MORES

FLORIDA·STATE·UNIVERSITY

1857

Tallahassee

FIRST WORLD, THIRD WORLD

cases in Vietnam no genuine surplus[56] for accumulation is produced at all, but given the ability of household plot production to enhance the subsistence of cooperative members, the existence of a surplus in the collective sector over and above the minimum subsistence needs of members is more likely. This is why household plots have been such a necessary feature of collective agriculture under the technologically backward conditions of Vietnam. Without them, such a high proportion of collective output would have to be distributed as necessary means of subsistence that a surplus could exist in very few places indeed and, in fact, in most cases cooperatives would be operating at considerable losses.

If the problem is looked at in this way, then expanded reproduction of agriculture is seen to be determined in the collective sector and, far from 'private' agriculture 'exploiting' the collective, the relationship is the reverse. In such a view, the household plot becomes the means by which the collective body is able to mobilise labour to produce means of subsistence in a way which reduces costs to the collective. This effect is increased where families are willing to apply labour to production in a much more intensive way than workers in the collective fields, leading to high output by comparison with the rather small area used.

The use of the 'product contract' system can be seen as an extension of this system of mobilising labour to the collective fields themselves, since it is envisaged as a means whereby the family can improve its subsistence level rather than a means for capital accumulation by individual households.[57] If we were to continue the analogy with capitalist farming, we might see the contract system as similar to the use of sharecropping as a way of enhancing the profitability of an enterprise under conditions of technologically backward farming methods by relating income of labourers more directly to effort expended than under the wage system (or workpoint system in the case of collectives) and thereby increasing productivity. It is possible to read too much into such analogies and it is important to be reminded here that the social relations of production of the two systems are quite different – in one case a system of social appropriation of the surplus is in operation (in which collective incentives also have a role), in the other case it is private. Nevertheless, the immediate purpose in both cases is to extract a surplus which can be utilised for expanded reproduction of the economy.

The contract system does raise the possibility, not present in the case of the five-per cent plots, of the accumulation of surpluses by individual households. One important way in which this can rise is through the existence of differential rent accruing to peasants who are allocated more fertile land. To overcome this, the Government initially ruled that lands would be redistributed every three years, but by 1988 this had come to be regarded as a fetter on peasant investment in maintaining and improving the fertility of soil, and contracts are now to be extended to ten years.[58] Such surpluses can lead to differential rates of accumulation and the eventual concentration of means of production in the hands of a minority of wealthy households. (This process was already well under way in South Vietnam by 1975 and arguably has not yet been brought under the domination of the socialist system.) The problem for the socialist regime is one of how best to assure social appropriation of these household surpluses without reducing the effectiveness of contracts as an incentive system. A number of options are open to increase social control over investible funds including, for example, taxation measures, pricing policy and encouraging farmers to deposit savings at banks, buy government bonds, etc. While such a system need not preclude family ownership of traditional means of production, the essential thing is to ensure that individual appropriation of surpluses produced by others is progressively eliminated: if very large household surpluses are allowed to amass, exploitation will inevitably reappear.

It is important to note also that contracting to households in Vietnam is intended to be confined to labour-intensive tasks (transplanting, tending, harvesting and sometimes ploughing with buffaloes).[59] Those aspects of production which have been mechanised, tractor-ploughing being the most widespread and obvious, have been retained by the collective and are done by teams organised at the brigade, cooperative or district level. Individual peasants are therefore now related to the collective institutions through a system of exchange of inputs and services for grain and other produce, rather than having the collective directly organise their work. Mechanisation is precisely the area from which it is expected that the main increase in labour productivity will come, and if the cooperative sector is to continue to provide the dynamic force in economic expansion it is necessary that such tasks should be retained by it. However, shortages of inputs such as fuel and electricity continue to affect the economic efficiency of mechanised farming and they also affect the ability of contractors to carry out their labour-intensive tasks with maximum effect, inhibiting the usefulness of the new incentives in increasing output and incomes. Some of these shortages are unavoidable in the short run, since they depend upon changes to the industrial structure and/or increased availability of imports.

We can argue then, that the cooperative sector remains dominant in Vietnamese agriculture, even though the main expansion of output appears to be occurring in the household sector, because it not only determines the existence of household agriculture – the family plots and contract land are allocated by the collective and do not exist independently from it – but it also fixes the limits of expansion of the household sector (via taxation policy, ownership and control of modern inputs and means of production). The use of individual incentives to mobilise labour for the production of means of subsistence on family plots, or to increase the output of the collective as a whole and enlarge its capacity to produce and mobilise a surplus for accumulation purposes (whether these be local or national) is something determined, not by the households themselves, but at the level of the social entity. Moreover, as long as these decisions are retained by the collective (or by the State), we cannot speak of a return to 'private property' in agriculture.

Indeed, the consolidation of social appropriation of surpluses was an explicit aim of the 1979 reforms. In introducing the decisions of the 6th Central Committee Plenum, Le Duan said:

> The state must control, by every available means, an increasingly large quantity of grain. ... To control grain, we must not use compulsory administrative inspections as has been done in the recent past at a number of places, rather, we must adopt correct policies regarding taxes, the stabilisation of obligations, two-way contracts and prices in order to insure that the state controls grain and provide incentive for farmers to eagerly produce grain and happily sell grain to the state.[60]

Thus we are not looking at a system in which two different 'modes of production' governed by different 'laws of motion' coexist either in a state of competition or interdependence. The 'laws of motion' are those of the socialist system. A parallel argument can be found in Lenin's writing on agricultural transformation under capitalism:

> Remember Marx's *Capital*. In it you will find references to the extreme variety of forms of land ownership, such as feudal, clan, communal (and primitive-squatter), state, etc., which capitalism encounters when it makes its appearance on the historical scene.

Capital subordinates to itself all these varied forms of landownership and remoulds them after its own fashion . . .[61]

A clear distinction is made here between the form of the relationship and its substance which has been subordinated to and remoulded by the dominant mode of production. In the same way, petty proprietorship in Northern Vietnam has been subordinated to and remoulded by socialism.

CONCLUSION

We may summarise the main conclusions of the argument presented above as follows:

(i) Until the late 1970s an implicit assumption of collectivisation in Vietnam was that an increase in the *scale* of agriculture was equivalent to the introduction of a new division of labour, in most cases still based on traditional techniques, on large-sized farms. I have tried to show here that this division of labour was artificial and did not cause economies of scale such that labour productivity rose – there was no *a priori* reason why it should.

(ii) In fact this kind of division of labour is more likely to introduce diseconomies in the absence of an incentive scheme which relates the income received by the cooperators directly to the effort expended on production. This effect arises because of the peculiar nature of the agricultural labour process, its spatial dispersion and need for considerable use of judgement by those involved, and problems of supervision and control of this process. (It would seem to be more in keeping with socialist principles to use incentives rather than supervision – with its attendant dangers of 'commandism' – to achieve the desired increase in productivity.) The workpoint system failed to achieve a close relationship between work effort and income precisely because there was no close relationship between completion of a set task and production of final output. Household-based production – on family plots and contract land – can be used as part of a system of incentives that is particularly appropriate where labour intensive techniques continue to be employed.

(iii) However, if social appropriation of economic surpluses is to remain a policy objective, these measures need to be undertaken in conjunction with reforms at the collective level and at the macroeconomic level. There need to be incentives for cooperatives to utilise accumulation funds effectively by providing better quality and range of inputs and services to farmers and this will involve both policies to overcome shortages at the macroeconomic level and to develop the system of exchange between collectives and the national economy, and policies to encourage efficient use of existing capacity at the micro level in order to develop the system of exchange between collective institutions and individual peasant cooperators.

Whereas in the more traditional view of the relationship between household and collective farming the problems of the collectives in failing to increase labour productivity are largely due to the expansion of the 'private' sector, the explanation advanced above suggests that it is precisely when household activity is encouraged that the collectives should thrive because they will have to devote less resources to subsistence and can utilise surpluses accruing for expanded reproduction and modernisation. Conversely, the use of administrative methods to restrict household market activity would be expected to have a detrimental effect on cooperatives by squeezing their profitability[62] and reducing their ability to participate in an expanded national market.

6 The Vietnamese Industrialisation Debate

Previous chapters have focused on the transformation of agriculture in the two halves of the country because it is still the most important sector in terms of employment and share of national income. We have seen how, in the South, revolutionary pressure between 1955 and 1975, transformed social relations and helped to establish a viable, family-based farming system similar to those of South Korea and Taiwan. With the seizure of political power in the South by the revolutionaries, the very different conditions prevailing in the rural areas, compared to North Vietnam in 1954, made the pattern of land reform followed fairly rapidly by collectivisation, less relevant and more difficult to implement without antagonising those whose earlier support had been the foundation of revolutionary success. These unfamiliar conditions in the South together with the problems in cooperative farming in the North inevitably led to fundamental rethinking of policy and eventual reform.

The changes in agriculture did not, however, occur in isolation from developments in the economy of the two regions as a whole. We have already seen, in Chapter 3, that in South Vietnam there existed a relatively sophisticated social division of labour based chiefly on the growth of aid-financed manufactured imports. This division of labour proved both advantageous and disadvantageous in the post-war situation. On the one hand, it rendered the Southern economy vulnerable to extreme dislocation when the US financial prop was withdrawn and the chain of commodity exchanges it had supported collapsed. On the other hand, the relative absence of village or regional economic autonomy in the South has provided a powerful stimulus for the re-establishment of commodity exchange on an expanded scale.

On the other hand, one of the basic tenets of Vietnamese thinking on economic unification was that Southern agricultural and light industrial potential would be complemented by the mineral and energy resources and heavy industrial capacity of the North. Northern industry had been expected to play an important role in offsetting the dislocating effects of American aid withdrawal and in allowing the state socialist sector of the North to seize the 'commanding heights' of the economy.

First World, Third World

William Ryrie

St. Martin's Press
New York

FIRST WORLD, THIRD WORLD

St. Martin's Press, Scholarly and Reference Division,
175 Fifth Avenue, New York, N.Y. 10010

First published in the United States of America in 1995

Printed in Great Britain

ISBN 0-312-15873-4

Library of Congress Cataloging-in-Publication Data applied for.

In reality, the Northern industrial sector was not well equipped to fulfil this role at the end of the war. Although considerable efforts were made to come to the aid of the South in the immediate aftermath,[1] this imposed an additional burden on a Northern population already living close to a minimum subsistence level. In this chapter we make a more detailed assessment of the industrial development of the DRV and ask why it was unable to play the dynamic role earlier expected of it. The theoretical premises of the VCP's development strategy are also examined. The problems inherent in the 'heavy industry first' strategy adopted in North Vietnam in the 1960s are already well known: they were canvassed in the 1920s industrialisation debate in the Soviet Union and have more recently come to light in the writings of various East European, Chinese and Soviet advocates of economic reform. Nevertheless, there has been a repeated tendency to return to this type of strategy in many socialist countries – despite rhetoric to the contrary. We shall therefore look at the reasons for this persistence and at ways in which, in Vietnam, the problem of integrating the South might lead to a more substantial modification of the policy of promoting new heavy industry in the medium to long term.

STRUCTURE OF THE DRV ECONOMY 1954–74

The economy inherited by the DRV from the French could hardly be described as industrialised. Though few reliable figures are available for the colonial period, Bernard did make some estimates for 1931 from which some idea of the structure of production in the three administrative sub-divisions of Vietnam can be gleaned (Table 6.1). Part A of the table shows that Tonkin was the most industrialised of the three zones. It should be remembered, however, that 1931 was in the middle of the Great Depression when prices of agricultural products were particularly low relative to industrial prices so that agriculture's share (in Part B) is therefore understated, compared with normal years.[2]

Modern industry (both mining and manufacturing) reportedly comprised about 10 per cent of material output in North Vietnam towards the end of the pre-war period, but wartime destruction between 1940 and 1954 and the fact that the French dismantled much of their industrial infrastructure prior to departure reduced this to 1.5 per cent by 1954.[3] The number of modern factories in operation in 1955 was only seven.[4] North Vietnam's most important export in the colonial period had been coal, but this was only about three per cent of total

Table 6.1 Structure of production in 1931, per cent

Sector	Tonkin	Annam	Cochin-China	Total
A. By region				
Agriculture, forestry, fishing	34.7	27.5	37.8	100.0
Industry	55.2	22.4	22.4	100.0
— modern	56.2	21.0	22.8	100.0
— handicraft	52.6	26.3	21.1	100.0
Services	34.5	17.2	48.3	100.0
Total	39.2	25.0	35.8	100.0
B. By sector				
Agriculture, forestry, fishing	57.2	71.2	68.2	64.7
Industry	30.9	19.6	18.1	21.9
— modern	23.1	13.5	14.7	16.1
— handicraft	7.8	6.1	3.4	5.8
Services	11.8	9.2	18.0	13.4
Total	100.0	100.0	100.0	100.0

Source P. Bernard, *Le Problème économique indochinois* (Paris: Nouvelles Éditions Latines, 1934) p. 14.

Indo-Chinese exports and estimates derived from Bernard's study suggest that all exports amounted to less than 10 per cent of Tonkin's total output (less than two per cent for Annam) compared with nearly 40 per cent in Cochin-China.[5] The picture at the end of the First Indo-China War is thus one of a rather autarkic agrarian economy, using traditional methods of cultivation, in which most industrial output – of consumer goods and farm tools – took place in the handicraft sector.

Tables 6.2 and 6.3 give some idea of the changes in this economic structure which came about over the succeeding two decades. Industry increased its share in output value until 1965 when its surge was temporarily reversed as a result of the heavy American bombing during 1965–8 and again in 1972. Nearly 30 per cent of the national income of the DRV came from industry in 1971. Agriculture declined slightly in importance up to 1965, but by the end of the decade had regained its earlier share. Though farm employment declined, it none the less remained by far the most important source of livelihood for the population (Table 6.3) and tended to be supplanted, not by industry, but by other sectors – chiefly trade and non-producing. We have

Table 6.2 Shares of national income by sector 1957–71, per cent

Year	Industry	Agri-culture and Forestry	Construc-tion	Commerce and Services	Transport and Communi-cations	Other	Total
1957	16.0	44.4	3.4	20.8	2.3	13.1	100.0
1960	18.2	42.3	4.7	20.5	2.8	11.5	100.0
1965	23.1	39.8	6.8	17.3	2.5	10.5	100.0
1968	19.9	43.9	6.4	16.4	2.4	11.0	100.0
1971	28.3	42.1	7.9	8.9	3.0	9.8	100.0

Source   G. Nguyen Tien Hung, *Economic Development of Socialist Vietnam, 1955–80* (New York: Praeger, 1977) p. 104.

Table 6.3 Structure of employment in the DRV

	1960	1965	1975
Industry	7.0	8.3	10.6
Construction	1.7	3.3	7.5
Agriculture and Forestry	83.0	78.6	64.7
Trade	3.0	2.3	3.1
Transport and Communications	1.2	1.7	2.2
Total material production	96.6	94.2	89.3
Non-material production	3.4	5.8	10.7

Source   A. Vickerman, 'Industry in Vietnam's Development Strategy', *Journal of Contemporary Asia,* vol. 15 (1985) no. 2, p. 230.

already seen in Chapter 5 that after 1968 the declining share of agricultural employment was not compensated by increases in labour productivity which could generate growth of rural per capita incomes and/or investible surpluses.

The structure of industrial production set out in Table 6.4 shows that during the first five years of the DRV industry was preponderantly concentrated in (a) production of consumer goods (Group B) rather than capital goods (Group A); (b) handicrafts rather than modern industry and (c) enterprises under local rather than central control. The predominance of Group B lasted throughout the period known as 'Reconstruction', until 1957, and that of 'Socialist Transformation', 1958–60. Rapid expansion in modern industry's share at this time was due to rebuilding of some of the war-damaged plant and equipment left behind by the French as well as by new investment carried out with Soviet and Chinese assistance.

Table 6.4 Structure of industrial production in the DRV 1955–75
(percentage of gross output value)

Year	Group A	Group B	Handi-craft	Modern industry	Central management	Local management
1955	27	73	71	29	12	88
1956	29	71	59	41	25	75
1957	24	76	57	43	28	72
1958	25	75	52	48	36	64
1959	32	68	46	54	48	52
1960	34	66	43	57	40	60
1961	–	–	41*	59*	–	–
1962	37	63	35	65	47	53
1963	39	61	33	67	48	51
1964	40	60	30	70	52	48
1965	43	57	26	74	54	46
1966	46	54	28	72	51	49
1967	44	56	31	69	45	55
1968	45	55	27	73	47	53
1969	–	–	–	–	–	–
1970	–	–	–	–	–	–
1971	41	59	24	76	49	51
1972	40	60	26	74	45	55
1973	42	58	27	73	44	56
1974	43	57	–	–	45	55
1975	43	57	–	–	51	49

Source   Vickerman, op. cit. p. 228; *Nguyen Tien Hung, op. cit., p. 98.

Changes in the distribution of industry between central and local management were also quite marked at this time, and reflect transfer of ownership as well as the concentration of investment in centrally-run industry shown in Table 6.5. Socialist transformation in ownership of the means of production was considered complete by 1960 with some form of collective farming affecting most peasants and the transfer of industry into State or (in the case of handicrafts) cooperative hands.

The Third Congress of the Vietnam Workers' Party in 1960 defined the next stage of development thus: 'the central task of the whole period of transition is socialist industrialisation, within which the key is the priority development of heavy industry.'[6] This policy was embodied in the First Five Year Plan (1961–5) and is reflected in the sharp rise in the investment share of Group A.

Whatever the DRV leaders' preferences, the path of development was upset by the commencement of US bombing. Aside from widespread destruction of industrial capacity caused by the bombing itself,

Table 6.5 Structure of investment in the DRV, per cent

		All Sectors			Industry			
	Agri-		*Industry*		*Group A*	*Group B*	*Central*	*Regional*
	culture	*Total*	*A*	*B*				
1955–57	15	31	20	11	66	34	100	–
1958–60	12	46	31	15	67	33	98	2
1961–64	21	53	41	12	78	22	94	6
1965–68	14	33	27	6	82	18	75	25
1969–71	21	40	30	10	76	24	75	25

Source Nguyen Tien Hung, op. cit., pp. 123, 142.

many factories had to be dismantled and removed to rural areas,
dispersing concentrations of production. Although this meant that
factories could continue operations, economies of scale were lost and
many other problems were encountered in removing established industries to remote areas which lacked infrastructure or an industrial
background. The hitherto rapid expansion of industry stopped and
indeed output declined in some sectors (Table 6.6). The industrial
structure of 1975 was very little different from that of 1965, though in
the recovery which followed the cessation of bombing and especially
after the signing of the Paris Peace Agreement in 1973, the centrally
managed and heavy industry sectors once again showed a tendency to
expand their shares. (Group A industries are more concentrated under
central control.)

The dramatic decline in the fortunes of all industrial sectors in the
wake of the escalation of war in 1965 is evident from Table 6.6.
Particularly hard hit were the sectors producing consumer goods

Table 6.6 Growth rates of industry by sector in the DRV (per cent per
annum at 1959 constant prices)

Year	Total	Group A	Group B	Industry	Handicraft	Central	Local
1955–59	42.6	49.1	39.9	66.6	27.9	101.2	25.3
1959–64	14.8	19.7	12.1	20.9	5.4	16.8	12.8
1964–68	–0.6	2.4	–2.8	0.3	–2.9	–3.1	1.9
1968–73	7.6	6.0	8.8	7.8	18.6	6.3	8.7
1973–75	15.8	–	–	–	–	23.8	9.4
1955–73	14.6	17.4	13.1	20.6	8.5	23.2	11.7

Source Calculated from Nguyen Tien Hung, op. cit., p. 140.

(Group B and handicrafts) and traditional implements of agriculture (handicrafts). A more disaggregated picture of the impact of war can be gained by looking at indices of production for some of the major products of North Vietnamese industry (Table 6.7). It has been chosen to start with 1957 rather than 1955 because by this time most industrial production in the DRV had regained pre-Second World War levels. Output volumes are measured against the base year of 1965, the last year before the effect of the bombing was fully felt.

The very high growth-rates for most of the industries listed in this table between 1957 and 1965 must be seen in the context of the low starting-point. However, of the 26 industries listed, at least nine suffered falls in output by 1968, and another six had 1970–1 output at or below 1965 levels. There were further falls in 1972, when the bombing was resumed and twelve still had not recovered their 1965 levels of output by the mid-seventies. Apatite ore, sugar and bicycle production appear to have declined continuously from 1965 to 1974. Of those industries in which 1970 output was higher than that of 1965, electrical transformers, ploughs and harrows, and rush mats, production had suffered a decline by 1974.

Only eleven of the 26 industries experienced average growth-rates of output in excess of 2.5 per cent per annum during 1965–74; that is, their per capita output remained steady or increased over the decade. They included electricity, chemical fertiliser, electric transformers, ploughs and harrows, livestock fodder, processing machinery, car tyres and tubes, rush mats, fish sauce, seasoning, cigarettes and salt, yet as we have already seen, two of these were experiencing difficulties in 1974.

As unification approached, therefore, North Vietnamese industry was in a state which would make it very difficult to carry out the leading role assigned to it by the 'economic complementarity' thesis and by orthodox socialist development theory. It is hard to avoid the conclusion, given the statistics for the years in which the major decline occurred, that the impact of the American escalation of the war was the cause of this. However, a number of other factors combined to ensure that, once peace was restored, a normal recovery based on the same overall development strategy would be extremely difficult.

'HEAVY INDUSTRY FIRST' IN THE POST-WAR CONTEXT

After a vigorous theoretical debate and political struggle which took place in the 1920s, the Soviet Union adopted an industrialisation

Table 6.7 Index of output of major industrial products 1957–74 (1965 = 100)

	1957	1965	1968	1970	1972	1974
Electricity, kWh	19	100	59	94	87	162
Coal, tonnes	26	100	57	64	40	88
Apatite ore, t	10	100	na	32*	29	22
Cement, t	29	100	12	91	27	61
Chrome, t	8	100	na	na	na	71
Machine tools, no.	–	100	na	100	na	110†
Diesel motors, no.	–	100	na	105	na	119
Electric transformers, no.	–	100	na	179	na	165
Pig iron, t	–	100	na	23	na	76
Timber, m³	40	100	66	80*	69	75
Car tyres and tubes, sets	–	100	na	90	na	138
Chemical fertiliser, t	16	100	83	126	124	238
Ploughs and harrows, no.	–	100	na	171	na	142
Livestock fodder processing machines, no.	–	100	na	25	na	150
Insecticide, t	–	100	na	93	na	109
Paper, t	10	100	37	62	46	82
Rush mats, pairs	125	100	na	158	na	128
Cloth, metres	67	100	83	89	73	96
Chinaware, pieces	–	100	na	113	na	123
Fish sauce, litres	493	100	na	na	na	74
Seasoning, t	–	100	na	319	na	635
Sugar, t	13	100	45	45*	42	37
Cigarettes, packs	11	100	100	131*	122	174
Soap, t	38	100	50	50*	62	83
Bicycles, no.	–	100	101	73*	72	45
Salt, t	72	100	113	129*	98	147

*1971; †1973.

Sources Nguyen Tien Hung, *Economic Development of Socialist Vietnam 1955–80* (New York: Praeger, 1977) p. 144; Vo Nhan Tri, *Croissance économique de la Republique démocratique du Viet Nam,* (Hanoi: Editions en Langues étrangères, 1967) p. 231; Vien Kinh Te Hoc, *35 Nam Kinh Te Viet Nam 1945–1980,* Hanoi: *Nha Xuat Ban Khoa Hoc Xa Hoi,* 1980, p. 97; *Vietnamese Studies,* no. 44, 1976, p. 210; General Statistical Office, *Tinh Hinh Phat Trien Kinh Te va Van Hoa Mien Bac Xa Hoi Chu Nghia 1960–1975,* Hanoi, 1978, pp. 80–2.

strategy which, in its essentials, provided a model for the socialist countries until at least the 1960s. The model presumed a rather autarkic economy and the political and economic feasibility of 'squeezing the peasantry' in order to maximise the agricultural surplus available for investment in industry, especially capital goods industry. Virtually all the socialist countries followed a policy of financing development from internal resources, ignoring comparative advantage in trade, establishing duplicate industrial structures and restricting consumption by manipulation of taxes, subsidies and rationing in order to increase the investment rate.[7] The theoreticians of such a strategy argued that the growth rate of industry depended upon the growth rate of the capital goods sector (the sector producing machinery and raw materials). In the short run, the high investment rate necessary to achieve growth in these more capital-intensive branches of industry would mean compression of the share of consumption. In the longer run, the development of industries capable of producing means of production would accelerate the overall growth rate of the economy and raise the level of consumption faster than under any alternative strategy.

Against such a strategy Soviet writers like Bukharin and Shanin argued that the high investment rates necessary to achieve growth in these more capital-intensive branches of industry would mean intolerable sacrifices of improvements in living standards. In order to retain political support of the peasantry, the opponents of 'heavy industry first' said that investment should be concentrated instead in light industry and agriculture. This would not only provide immediate relief to the population, but could also expand export income enabling the purchase of needed industrial capital equipment abroad at a lower price. The growth rate of the economy could, realistically, be expected to be no higher than the rate of growth of the sectors producing consumer goods (both for the domestic and export markets).

Compression of the consumption share does not in itself entail stagnating or declining per capita consumption levels.[8] But this is so only if labour productivity in agriculture (the consumer goods sector) rises and the marketed surplus over and above peasant consumption requirements also rises, enabling an expansion of employment in the capital goods sector. The marketed surplus of agriculture therefore provides a fundamental constraint (unless there are aid-financed food imports) to the growth rate of real consumption. In a country like Vietnam, in which population is growing at over two per cent per annum, productivity increases in agriculture become doubly important.

This immediately suggests two things: (i) that in an economy with a severe foreign exchange bottleneck, the output of the capital goods sector needs to be directed in the first instance towards providing modern inputs to boost the productivity of agriculture (and industries producing necessary consumer goods) and (ii) that care is needed to ensure both that agricultural labour is organised in a way that maximises its effectiveness and that peasant incentives to produce a marketed surplus are adequate. Moral incentives may have some application here, particularly in the case of Vietnam in encouraging peasants to contribute to the war effort, but in the long run increasing supplies of consumer goods (both collective and individual) will be required. While it may also be thought possible to expand marketed surpluses by coercion or 'administrative methods', this can lead to falling labour productivity–especially in agriculture where individual farmers retain a high degree of control over the labour process. Ultimately, it can lead to slow growth or even falling national income.

Thus the factors influencing the productive effect of a given quantity of investment are the main determinants of the extent to which the level of per capita consumption restricts the rate of investment out of national income. If per capita consumption is too high, the transition period required to reach a full employment growth-path can stretch to infinity.[9] Thus the danger for a very poor economy which already suffers from high population growth-rate, low per capita consumption levels and high unemployment is that unless the effectiveness of investment can be improved and/or access to external resources can increase the total pool of income, either declining per capita consumption or a declining rate of investment will perpetuate the state of underdevelopment indefinitely.

Key elements in improving investment effectiveness are Kalecki's 'a' and 'u' factors[10] relating to the rate of depreciation of the capital stock and the extent to which elimination of wastage, more effective use of existing production capacity, reorganisation of labour resources, etc. can be attained, and the question of maintaining proportionality between different sectors (for example, between sectors producing machines to make machines, machines to make consumer goods, and the consumer goods sector itself). Here again, however, the system of resource allocation embodies a system of incentives for enterprise managers and workers: if these are not effective any new organisation of production and investment will also be ineffective.

Trade is a very important way in which investment effectiveness can be improved and the need to compress consumption minimised. By expanding markets for domestically produced goods, trade enables producers to take advantage of economics of scale and utilise existing comparative advantage to achieve a rapid increase in export income. Higher export income means improved access to cheaper and better quality capital goods and manufactured consumer goods than are available locally–in most cases the size of the domestic market is too small to enable capital goods industries to reap economies of scale and the result is that costs are high and the investment rate required to construct planned industries excessive.

Few figures are available on the foreign trade of the DRV. However, we do know that the regime did not adopt an export-orientated growth strategy. It saw the key to economic growth as lying in the construction of a capital goods sector, as we saw above, and relatively few resources were devoted to those sectors which might have produced big increases in export income (primary products). Export growth lagged behind growth of the total social product. The share of unprocessed agricultural products fell from 28 per cent of the total in 1960 to eight per cent in 1974, or little over half of their 1960 value.[11] The mining of coal, which had been an important pre-war export, was badly affected by the bombing and the growth rate of output lagged behind the rest of the economy. An effective transport network is also necessary for the expansion of exports and this was a key area which suffered from American bombing in the 1960s: for example railway passenger traffic fell by 81 per cent, between 1964 and 1967.[12]

Foreign aid also enables per capita consumption to be raised during the period of transition to full employment growth (which can also be shortened) in so far as the effect of aid is also to maintain an investment rate sufficient to ensure growth. This has had a two-edged effect in the Vietnamese case. On the one hand, it enabled development during the war years of a heavy industrial base without requiring the serious consumption sacrifices from the population which would otherwise have been necessary. This was just as well, because the need to finance the war effort and the already low subsistence level of most Vietnamese would otherwise have made such an industrialisation strategy an intolerable burden. On the other hand, the end of the war in 1975 saw a change in both the amount and type of economic assistance available and this has had important consequences for the recovery from wartime damage. The subsequent foreign exchange shortage has served to emphasise the key role of improving investment effectiveness if a high growth-rate is to be achieved.

The importance of such considerations to Vietnam is brought out by figures on per capita production of basic consumer goods – for example food and textiles – which are used here as a proxy for consumption of these goods. These are set out in Table 6.8 and give some idea of the narrow constraints operating on investment policy in the post-war period. Any growth strategy involving reductions in per capita consumption ran the risk of forcing large sections of the population below

Table 6.8 Average annual per capita production of food and cloth
(geographical territory of DRV)

Year	Paddy kg	Staple grains kg	Cloth metres
1939	211	228	–
1955–59	293	367	3.57
1960–64	261	373	5.17*
1965–68	220	342	–
1969–73	204	308	3.24†

(–) Indicates insufficient data; * Excludes 1961; †1972 and 1973 only.
Sources Le Chau, *Le Vietnam Socialiste,* pp. 217, 219; Hung, op. cit.,
p. 127, 144; Kai Carlberg and Jens-Christian Sorensen, 'Landbruget i den
vietnamesiske udviklingsstrategi', *Den Ny Verden,* vol. 14, (1980) no. 1,
p. 79.

the minimum physical subsistence level, not only impairing labour
productivity, but posing a potential threat to political support for the
regime, particularly among the peasantry.

Minimum subsistence consumption of rice in Vietnam is generally
considered to be 240 kg of paddy (unhusked rice) per annum. The
ability of the domestic rice harvest to provide this amount was
precarious and, except for the period 1955–64, the average diet must
have included either secondary grain crops like maize, sweet potato and
cassava, or imported grain. Grain imports did increase sharply after
1968.[13] Even in its first decade, the DRV produced barely enough if
requirements for stocks and seed and loss through waste or pests are
taken into account.

Estimates of foreign aid to the North Vietnamese economy from the
socialist countries during 1955–65 show a total of nearly $US1 billion
over the 11-year period.[14] Sixty-four per cent of this took the form of
loans which increased in significance during the latter part of the
period, as did the importance of the Soviet Union as a lender. Most aid
came from China (50.2 per cent), followed by the Soviet Union (40.1
per cent), with Chinese grants being the most important source during
the early 'Reconstruction' phase. Nguyen Tien Hung cites US estimates
for Soviet aid as being in the range of $US345–360 million in 1970 and
$US315–450 million in 1971.[15] He also estimates Chinese aid at $100
million per annum in the early 1970s. Other estimates of $US 1778
million and $US 1491 million from the USSR and China respectively
for the period 1965–75, suggest somewhat lower total aid levels.[16]

For the early years (1955–60), foreign aid ranged between 40.7 per cent of budget expenditure and 17.8 per cent.[17] The planned share of foreign aid in total investment expenditure in 1958–60 was 62 per cent falling to 35 per cent in 1961–5.[18] The lesser importance of external assistance in investment and budget expenditure in the sixties reflects the growing ability of North Vietnamese industry to provide internal accumulation funds. Thus in 1955, the agricultural tax raised 30.6 per cent of budget revenue and the industrial enterprise tax only 6.5 per cent. In 1959, agricultural tax was responsible for only 9.3 per cent and the enterprise tax for 52.2 per cent. The main burden had shifted from foreign aid plus agriculture, to industry plus foreign aid.[19] No firm data are available, but the estimates of increased aid levels combined with stagnating industrial production after the escalation of war in 1965 suggest a greater reliance on foreign aid from that date.

The capital goods content of foreign aid to the DRV was rather high. For 1955–9 the share of means of production (fixed capital only) ranged from 43 to 63 per cent, while that of consumption goods (including intermediate goods) fell from nearly 50 per cent to 18 per cent. In 1955–7 consumer goods formed the higher proportion of this group, whereas in 1958–9 raw materials came to dominate. From 1960 to 1964 intermediate goods are included under means of production and this category took well over 90 per cent of foreign aid, while consumer goods imports were reduced nearly to zero (the balance consisted of services).[20] The policy followed in the DRV therefore stands in sharp contrast to that followed in the South where capital and intermediate goods were 60 per cent of imports financed by the Commercial Import Program betwee.1 1960 and 1964 and consumer goods 40 per cent.[21] After 1964 there are no data from the North on the commodity composition of aid, but a rough indication can be gained by looking at the overall composition of imports. For 1960 the share of consumer goods was 13 per cent, for 1964, 22.2 per cent and for 1974, 32.2 per cent.[22] For the South, the comparable figure for 1965–72 was 48 per cent.[23]

On the basis of the limited data available, it seems that the high rates of growth experienced by the North Vietnamese economy were significantly fuelled by injections of foreign aid, enabling industrial investment to rise without too much detriment to per capita consumption levels.[24] From 1955 to 1965 food production rose fast enough to keep ahead of population growth and although after 1965 per capita food production fell, forcing a rise in consumer goods imports, there was no let-up in the heavy industry priority of the development strategy.

In North Vietnam, attempts to increase productivity of the agricultural sector primarily revolved round the setting-up of cooperatives, reorganisation of the labour supply, and use of labour accumulation projects to raise cropping intensity and land yields; that is, extensive use of Kalecki's 'u' factor to achieve a higher growth rate for a small capital expenditure. This was expected to generate marketable surpluses to assist both expansion of industry and the industrialisation of agriculture itself. However, the concentration of investment in the construction of 'heavy industry' and relative neglect of consumer goods carried with it the strong danger that the rise in agricultural productivity would run out of steam when peasants could no longer translate increased output into a higher standard of living. This danger could be averted to some extent during the war, not only by the willingness on the part of the population to make sacrifices for the cause of national reunification and independence, but also by the ability of the Government to subsidise consumption levels via foreign aid (chiefly imports of Chinese rice and manufactured consumer goods). Under peacetime conditions, however, and with reduced levels of foreign aid, this neglect of the consumption goods sector would become a key bottleneck, resulting in unacceptable reductions in per capita consumption. Peasants' retreat into autarky and shortages of food and raw materials in the urban sector would cause declining industrial productivity and lead to stagnation of national income, in spite of continuing high investment rates.

DISPROPORTIONALITY

The contribution of a given quantity of investment to growth of output depends upon a number of factors which can be divided basically into two camps: on the one hand are factors affecting labour productivity at the level of the firm and, on the other hand, factors related to balance in the economy, notably, the extent to which investment affects proportionality (input–output relationships). The two factors cannot be separated in practice because those affecting productivity (incentive systems, for example) have consequences for the supply of means of production and consumer goods, while the availability of these goods in turn affects productivity. In my view the disproportions which have characterised the Vietnamese economy in the wake of the war have been fundamental to its subsequent economic performance.

The analysis of disproportionality is based on Marx's reproduction schemes in Volume II of *Capital*. Through these schemes Marx analysed the conditions necessary for an economy to achieve an equilibrium growth-path – one ensuring that capital goods and wage goods were produced in the correct proportions to ensure replacement of worn-out and used up inputs as well as a supply of new capital and wage goods for the economy to grow. Although Marx's schemes were devised for a capitalist economy, the fundamental relationships established between producer goods and wage goods also hold for any other type of economy and have been taken up by socialist economists. This is not to say that the factors causing disproportions are the same for the different types of economic system.

In both capitalist and socialist economies, equilibrium (or proportional) growth has rarely, if ever, been achieved. It is well known that capitalism is characterised by economic crises of 'overproduction' (that is, overproduction in relation to effective demand). The characteristic disproportionality of socialism, on the other hand, is 'under-production' or shortage of goods relative to the demand for them.

The author who first drew attention to the problem of proportionality in the context of the Soviet industrialisation debates was Bukharin:[25]

> Our economic organs have not yet understood the absolutely urgent necessity of a thorough and thoughtful study of the structure of demand for industrial products, even though its significance from the viewpoint of analysis of reproduction is completely exceptional.

According to Bukharin's estimates, approximately 23–25 per cent of demand for industrial products in the Soviet Union came from the peasantry and three-quarters came from within the industrial sector itself. These proportions were significant in the context of the argument of the 'superindustrialisers' that the 'goods famine' being experienced in the Soviet Union was caused by the lag of industrial growth behind peasant demand. But, Bukharin pointed out, 'even industry itself, which is developing at record rates of growth, also has a furious demand for industrial products, but it cannot satisfy it . . . it turns out that industry "lags" behind itself'.[26]

Industry, according to Bukharin, had run into limits of development:

> (1) Clearly we have selected insufficiently correct relationships between the branches of industry itself (for instance, the clear lag of metallurgy). (2) It is clear that we have chosen insufficiently correct relationships between the growth of capital construction (both in

industry and in the socialised sector as a whole). If there are no bricks and if they cannot be produced in a given season (for technical reasons) beyond a certain amount, then one cannot draw up programs of construction which exceed that limit and create thereby a demand which cannot be satisfied ... (3) It is also clear that the limits of development are given by the output of raw materials: cotton, hides, wool, flax, etc., cannot be obtained from thin air ... these objects are the products of agricultural production, and their shortage is a cause of the insufficient development of the gross output of industry.[27]

Mao Zedong also took up these considerations in his famous essay 'On Ten Great Relations' (1956), which, however, hardly formed the basis for Chinese development strategy as practised after that date and has only been revived since the author's death. Mao's main concern in this essay was that heavy industry (loosely, and not entirely accurately, equated in official socialist literature with the capital goods sector or Marx's Department I) should be constructed on the basis of expansion in 'light industry' (that is, consumer goods) and agriculture. This embodies an incomplete view of the problem of proportionality, but it is consistent with the highly abstract, two-sector model of Marx's schemes and also shares one of the main concerns of Bukharin, namely, the so-called 'economic link' between industry and agriculture which, he felt, was the basis not only of the worker-peasant alliance, but of economic development under the historically given conditions of the Soviet economy.[28]

From the point of view of economic growth, the 'economic link' between agriculture and industry did not consist merely of extraction of an economic surplus from the rural sector in order to finance accumulation in industry (although this was also an important aspect). For Bukharin, a most important element of the link was the development of commodity exchange relations between the two sectors. On the one hand, agriculture, via its marketed surplus, would provide wage goods, raw materials and exports whose foreign exchange earnings could be used to purchase needed capital equipment. On the other hand, industry would provide manufactured inputs and capital equipment to raise the technological level of agriculture (acknowledged to be among the most backward in Europe). Industry would also provide consumer goods, not only to improve rural living standards, but also as an incentive for the peasantry to continue expanding their output and incomes. (This view of the exchange between industry and agriculture has been echoed time and again by Vietnamese sources.)

Those participants in the debate who concentrated exclusively on the problem of surplus extraction and failed to pay attention to the problem of *expanding peasant output and income* were, according to Bukharin, embarking on a self-defeating course: the failure of the New Economic Policy (NEP) in the Soviet Union to increase the ability of the Government to mobilise surplus agricultural output was due, not to *kulak* (sabotage), but to the shortage of industrial goods caused by the too rapid rate of investment in heavy industry.

Bukharin's theme here has also been taken up by the Hungarian economist, J. Kornai, who has argued that shortage is endemic to administratively planned economies.[29] In this view shortage (or 'under-production') is a self-reinforcing tendency in these economies. The high rates of investment and 'tight' planning norms create demands for resources which are impossible to satisfy. In the initial stages of development this may be due to bottlenecks caused by poor transport facilities, teething problems with new plant and equipment, inexperienced workforce, etc., or planning norms which exceed the actual output capacity of the economy. The existence of shortages will lead enterprise managers to over-order and hoard resources – particularly raw materials and spare parts, but also labour if this is scarce. The practice of hoarding in turn leads to considerable waste of productive capacity as well as reinforcing the shortage of available products relative to the demand for them. It also means that output grows less rapidly than planned, thereby leading to even higher growth and investment targets in the next period – reinforcing the tendencies which generated the shortage. Moreover, because large amounts of resources are tied up in heavy industry in the effort to achieve a more rapid expansion of industrial capacity, exacerbated by tendencies to hoard labour within enterprises, consumer demand tends to rise faster than the ability of the consumption goods sector to meet it.

Kornai leaves it to the reader to speculate upon what this might mean for the political stability of the socialist regime – though it is perhaps not surprising that many regard the introduction of market-type reforms in Eastern Europe as a response to a 'political cycle' whereby worker dissatisfaction with the rate of progress in improving living standards is met by, at least temporary, reductions in investment in heavy industry and efforts to bring production of consumer goods more into line with demand.[30]

The replacement of administrative planning, which confers economic power on the bureaucracy, can be achieved by the use of market forces as economic levers or even by 'loose' planning norms which leave more room for initiative and manoeuvre to individual managers, production groups or households. Such measures can, however, lead to another sort of political difficulty, especially among those whose control over resources is threatened. It is to be expected, then, that after a period of reform there will be pressure from the bureaucracy to revert to administrative planning methods and 'heavy industry first'.

In other words, there can be a cyclical movement between, on the one hand, high investment rates and priority to heavy industrial development and, on the other, reduced or stabilised rates of investment (which imply reduced rates of growth for heavy industry), and more rapid expansion of consumer goods output, that is, movement towards restoration of proportionality (or equilibrium) in the economy.

Bukharin regarded the question of proportionality as fundamental to planned economic growth. Indeed he stated in 'Notes of an Economist' that the establishment of balance between the different sectors was the same thing as drawing up a plan. He accepted that disproportionality was a part and parcel of the growth process, however, and argued that only by planning could a *tendency* to equilibrium be ensured without leading to *crises*.[31] Capitalism, on account of its unplanned, anarchic character, was inevitably plagued by crises. It was only by the process of devaluation of capital which occurred in the crisis that equilibrium could be restored. In a socialist economy, disequilibria caused by underproduction could be remedied by conscious planning of investment and output, based on establishing the correct input–output relations of the economy.

Preobrazhensky, as the leading theoretician of the so-called Left Opposition, was not in disagreement with this position,[32] though he had also argued that 'socialist primitive accumulation' should be based on unequal exchange between industry and agriculture in order to maximise surplus extraction from the latter. The difference between him and the Bukharinists lay in their respective attitudes towards the proportions which should be established between industry and agriculture, that is, the extent to which the peasantry should share in the benefits of expanded reproduction. Using Lenin's aphorism that 'politics is the concentrated expression of economics', Bukharin saw Preobrazhensky's position as amounting to narrow 'trade unionism' (although given that industry was also seen to 'lag behind itself', this label is illogical – neither side in the debate saw the dynamics of the socialist economy in terms of a cyclical movement brought about by tension between planners and workers/peasants). Bukharin's own position stressed the political importance of the worker-peasant alliance (calculated to win the compliance, if not active support, of the predominantly non-Bolshevik peasantry).

The early Soviet debates and some more recent contributions dealing with the same themes have been discussed at some length here because it is important not to attribute too much originality to Chinese or Vietnamese solutions to the problems raised by their industrialisation processes. The fact that virtually identical debates and struggles over industrialisation priorities have taken place in countries as diverse as the Soviet Union, Hungary, China, Cuba and Vietnam is itself significant in showing the *intractability* of certain economic problems in socialist countries. Once we see this, it becomes easier to distinguish those features which are systematically reproduced in socialist economies from those which are due to the specific characteristics of an individual economy.

Successful Communist Parties in China and Vietnam have, in contrast to the Bolsheviks in Russia, had a firm base within the peasantry. They have adopted economic strategies far more sympathetic to their peasant constituency than did the Bolsheviks under Stalin – collectivisation was undertaken with a minimum force (as distinct from land reforms which were accompanied by some retribution against wealthier rural classes), there have been no forced migrations and no systematic repression against the rural population. This has been made possible by the reservoir of goodwill established among the peasantry following rent reduction, land reform, food distribution, certain minimum welfare provisions such as medical treatment, child care and educational facilities and subsidies extended to guarantee peasants' livelihoods. But on the whole, the policies pursued in both China and Vietnam have focused on high rates of investment in the heavy industrial sector with comparatively little attention paid to the expansion of agricultural and consumer goods output – in spite of rhetoric to the contrary. In both cases, there have been cyclical movements as described above, but prior to the late 1970s, any retreat from 'priority to heavy industry' has been shortlived. The extent of such a retreat is conditioned by economic as well as political factors – the one being dependent upon the other.

The economic factor involved here is the extent of the disproportionalities between industry and agriculture, between heavy and light industry (or, more accurately, between means of production and consumer goods industries)[33] and, at a more disaggregative level, between the inputs and outputs of individual industries. The political factor is the extent to which such disproportionalities bring about dissatisfaction among sections of the population having varying political strengths. However, it is also inherently difficult to retreat from a 'heavy industry first' strategy because of the quantity of resources already tied up in large-scale projects. Some projects may have to be scrapped as a result of a shift in investment priorities and this adjustment will have its own costs.

Actual evidence of disproportionalities in the Vietnamese economy during the late 1970s is not difficult to obtain, but for the most part remains fragmentary. We have already noted the problems caused by falling agricultural production and the consequent food shortages in urban areas. Complaints of the low rate of capacity utilisation of industry also became frequent from 1978 onwards and a major cause of this was seen to be shortages of raw materials.

An article in *Giao Thong Van Tai* for September 1979, for example, pointed to a critical shortage of coal and other supplies for the railways which had forced the cancellations of three trains during the previous month. Only 40–60 per cent of supplies needed were getting through.[34] In the cement industry, capacity utilisation was reportedly only 20 per cent during 1981 because of raw material and energy shortages.[35]

Ho Chi Minh City machine enterprises complained of loss of production time of between 20 and 40 per cent due to delays in the supply of raw materials and power failures during 1979.[36] In the Marine Products Sector during 1979 an estimated 30 per cent of fishing boats were unusable due to shortages of spare parts and new engines.[37] During 1981, only 10 per cent of refrigerated storage capacity could be used due to power and raw material shortages.[38] In March 1980, *Nhan Dan* reported widespread shortages of agricultural tools: whereas annual production plans stipulated an annual output equal to 25 per cent of existing stock, only 10 per cent was in fact produced. The average ratios of ploughs and harrows to buffaloes of 0.7 and 0.3 respectively were half of what they were in 1977.[39]

Shortages in the consumer goods sector also occurred. For example in January 1980 *Nhan Dan* reported on the soap shortage: although enough vegetable oil was produced to suffice for 20 000 tonnes of soap per annum, centrally managed factories operated at only eight per cent of capacity and could only purchase five per cent of the total oil output due to hoarding by localities for handicraft production to meet local needs, competition between purchasing agencies which led to price increases and inability of the state purchasing agencies to provide adequate supplies of goods to farmers under the two-way contract system, leading to diversion of oil onto the free market.[40]

The central Light Industry Sector operated four machine enterprises in 1978 to produce spare parts. Capacity of just over 1800 tonnes per annum was expected to meet demand of over 3000 tonnes, although in 1978 actual production was only 1588 tonnes and much was of poor quality due to lack of adequate equipment. The light industry sector in general suffered from irregular supplies and variable quality of raw materials. In 1978 capacity utilisation in the plastic products branch was between 10 and 15 per cent, in laundry detergent 30 per cent and in soap manufacture 15 per cent while labour productivity was stagnant due to lack of essential maintenance work, failure to carry out capital-deepening investment and other shortages.[41] In 1981, capital utilisation in the sugar industry reportedly stood at 30 per cent and in the tobacco industry 20 per cent, due to shortages of raw material and energy.[42]

In August 1979 it was reported that few of the noodle factories in Ho Chi Minh City were operating and in Tay Ninh province 113 manioc processing factories were experiencing difficulties in obtaining raw materials due to poor transport facilities and many had ceased operation altogether.[43]

An article on the fishing industry in Kien Giang province in *Nhan Dan* in March 1980 reports a fall in the catch from 95 000 tonnes in 1976 to 50 000 tonnes in 1979. In the latter year, only 85 per cent of the state purchase target was met and 36 per cent of the export target. Three main causes were assigned: firstly, the loss of boats to 'escapees'; secondly, the shortage of new boats – although 6000 cubic metres of timber were allocated in the plan, only 300 had been delivered – and spare parts; thirdly, a change in management policy. Before 1978, all fish were unloaded at the provincial capital of Rach Gia where processing facilities had been established under the Thieu regime. Even boats from as far afield as Saigon would deliver their fish there. In 1978 all boats of less than 20 hp were assigned to the districts which often lacked adequate piers and processing facilities. While fish rotted at these sites, factories at Rach Gia, on the other hand, lacked sufficient raw material. The necessity to transport new boats and spares from Rach Gia to the districts created new complications and the districts acquired a 'self-sufficient, self-production, self-consumption' mentality as a result.[44]

These reports on the problems facing different industries add up to a picture of widespread and serious imbalances between output and effective demand. Acute disproportions existed both in the production of raw materials and spare parts relative to the manufacturing capacity of the economy and in supplies of consumer goods (especially agricultural products) relative to the requirements of reproducing an expanding labour force.

That these disproportions were serious enough during 1978–81 to amount to an economic crisis is indisputable. The crisis was triggered by the decline in agricultural output: whereas the real value of agricultural output grew by 10 per cent in 1976, the first full year of peace, it fell by five per cent in 1977, and did not recover in 1978. Growth resumed again in 1979 at an average real annual rate of five to six per cent between 1979 and 1984. Real value of livestock production fell in 1978 and did not recover until 1981.[45] As I have pointed out in earlier chapters, this decline resulted in a sharp fall in the share of grain output sold or transferred to the state, from 15 per cent in 1975 to 10 per cent in 1979 – even after recovery of total output had begun.

Falling grain output and state difficulties in mobilising the marketed surplus created problems for urban workers forcing them to turn to the free market for food supplies. High prices prevailing in the free market rendered urban wages and salaries utterly inadequate to sustain a minimum standard of living and so the phenomena of 'moonlighting', taking extra jobs, diversion of state property into the free market (for example, using state construction materials for private building jobs) became commonplace. Absence from work on 'other business' was allegedly responsible for the loss of 18 per cent of potential labour-days in the Ho Chi Minh City machinery sector during 1979.[46] These factors had enormous implications for industrial labour productivity as workers devoted their time and energy to the more lucrative free market activities. As labour productivity fell, output of key industrial products suffered, worsening the shortages.

The decline in agricultural output was also responsible for some of the shortages being experienced in industry. Per capita output of some major domestically produced industrial raw materials in 1979, as compared with earlier years, is shown in Table 6.9. For most of the agricultural products listed, there had been little improvement in supply since 1975.

The crisis in the state-run industrial sector was severe. Changes in output over the period 1975–84 are depicted in Figures 6.1–6.5. These show that, in most industrial sectors there was a decline in output in 1977–9, reaching a trough in 1980 or 1981 and, with a few exceptions, recovering thereafter. Real gross value of industrial output, after growing at over nine per cent per annum from 1975–8, fell by 4.5 per

Table 6.9 Per capita output of raw materials 1965–79

	1965	1970	1975	1979
Coal (kg)	121.0	66.0	110.0	106.0
Timber (m³)	0.04	0.03	0.03	0.04
Cement (kg)	21.8	13.1	11.3	13.4
Sea food (kg)	11.8	13.7	11.5	9.3
Salt (kg)	9.1	7.8	7.9	9.8
Jute (kg)	0.6	0.5	0.5	0.5
Peanuts (kg)	2.3	1.8	1.4	1.5
Tobacco (kg)	0.4	0.3	0.3	0.3
Sugarcane (kg)	52.8	21.6	34.4	65.5
Tea (kg)	0.3	0.3	0.4	0.4
Rubber (kg)	1.8	0.8	0.5	0.8

Source Danh Son, 'Raw Materials in the Effort to Build and Perfect the Production Structure in Our Country', *Nghien Cuu Kinh Te*, no. 6, November–December 1981, translated in JPRS 80671, *Vietnam Report*, no. 2361, p. 25.

cent and 9.6 per cent in 1979 and 1980 respectively. Recovery began in 1980 with a real annual growth rate of 19.4 per cent to 1982 and 11.1 per cent from 1982–4.

Out of 23 major industries for which data are available, in three (electricity, sugar, and ploughs and harrows) the recession was no more than a hiccup. Sixteen suffered a more or less serious decline beginning in 1977, 1978 or 1979 attributable to four major causes:

(1) declining agricultural output and marketed surplus affecting the supply of raw materials and food to industry;

(2) rising tension and then war with China leading to (a) the exodus of much of the ethnically-Chinese skilled workforce of North Vietnam,[47] as well as the more commercially orientated Chinese from the South, (b) the cessation of trade with and aid from China – estimated at 38 per cent of all foreign aid to the SRV in 1977[48] – and (c) direct war damage;[49]

(3) the US blockade and exhaustion of supplies of raw material and spare parts left over from the old regime in the South, and the beginning of a period of restructuring as industries began to seek new sources of supply, to retool in order to accommodate new or inferior quality (domestically produced) raw materials, and scrapping or idleness of unworkable capacity;

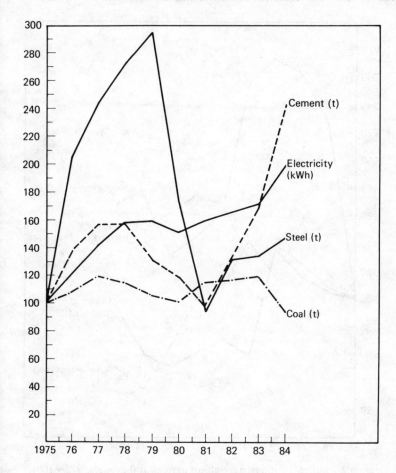

Figure 6.1   Indices of industrial output: heavy industry (1975 = 100)
Sources   *So Lieu Thong Ke,* 1979, pp. 32–3; 1982, pp. 32–3; 1984, pp. 44–5.

(4)   over-optimistic planning norms which, by generating shortages and wasted resources, in the manner described earlier in this section, slowed down the rate of growth.

None of these effects is individually quantifiable, and some are largely or partly beyond the control of the Government – the poor weather conditions in the late 1970s, the hostile international environment which affected points (2) and (3) above. The situation was exacerbated

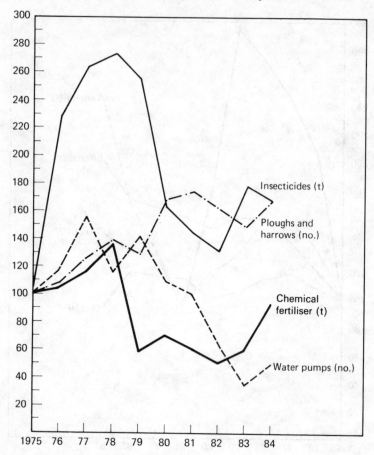

Figure 6.2   Indices of industrial output: agricultural inputs (1975 = 100)
Sources   As for Figure 6.1.

rather than improved, however, by the policies pursued by the Vietnamese Government at this time, in particular by the setting of over-ambitious goals.

Table 6.10 gives an indication of the thinking in 1976 about how rapidly the Vietnamese economy could be expected to develop in the period of the Second Five Year Plan (1976–80). Targets for most products in 1980 involved at least doubling (and sometimes trebling or quadrupling) of 1975 output, implying annual growth rates of over 15 per cent. The gross over-estimation of possibilities is partly explained, perhaps, by an optimistic evaluation of international events: the

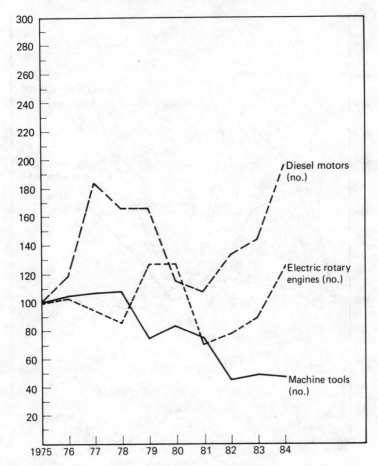

Figure 6.3   Indices of industrial output: engineering (1975 = 100)
Sources   As for Figure 6.1.

Vietnamese expected at that time to receive reconstruction aid from the USA[50] as well as the USSR, and it was also difficult to foresee the extent to which relations with China would deteriorate. There was too an over-optimistic assessment of the probability of finding and commencing oil production off shore within five years.[51]

STRUCTURAL ADJUSTMENT AND ECONOMIC RECOVERY

Changing the structure of capital formation and altering that of

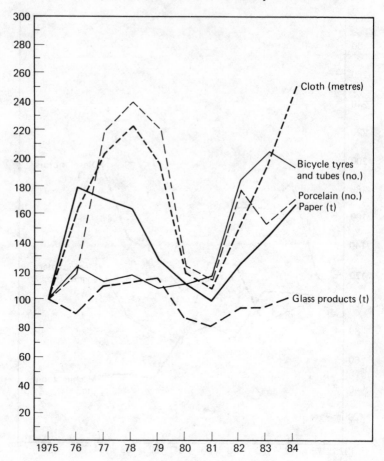

Figure 6.4   Indices of industrial output: consumer goods (1975 = 100)
Sources   As for Figure 6.1.

production are two inescapable components of growth. As I have already mentioned in connection with the debates over industrial policy in other socialist countries, all policies to increase the rate of growth are exercises in 'unbalanced' growth, and from this point of view the 'Bukharinists' and the 'superindustrialisers' are not different in their objectives. However, there are serious differences between the rival schools as to *how much* imbalance between industry and agriculture, urban and rural, modern and traditional sectors can be tolerated. The debates that have emerged around this topic are also debates about the economic system itself – between 'administrative planners', on the one

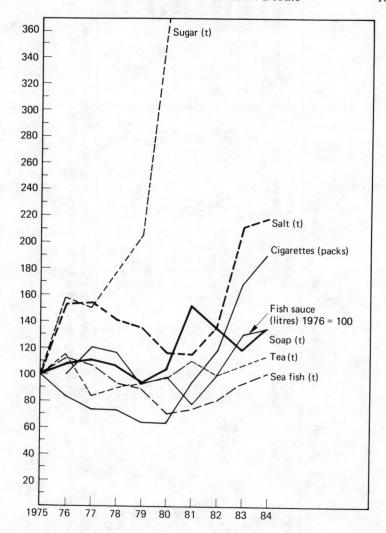

Figure 6.5   Indices of industrial output: processing of agricultural products (1975 = 100)
Sources   As for Figure 6.1.

hand, and those favouring an incentive-driven system, on the other. Thus it is not only a debate about the need to revise plan targets to obtain a new structure of production and capital accumulation in response to the crisis of industry, but about ways to ensure a permanent shift in the methods of setting social investment priorities which could

Table 6.10 Economic plans and performance 1976–85

Industry	1975 Actual (1)	1980 Plan (2)	1980 Actual (3)	(3)/(2) % (4)	1985 Plan (5)	1985 Actual (6)	(6)/(5) % (7)	Growth rates	
								1975–80 %	1980–85 %
Foodgrain m. t	11.6	21.0	14.4	68	19–20	18.2	94	4.4	4.8
Sea fish m. t	0.55	1.0	0.38	38	0.47–0.5	0.57	119	–7.1	8.4
Pigs m. head	9.2	16.5	10.0	61	13	11.8	91	1.7	3.4
Washed coal m. t	5.2	10.0	5.3	53	8–9	5.4	61	0.4	0.4
Electricity bn. kWh	2.4	5.0	3.7	74	5.5–6	5.2	89	9.0	7.0
Cement m. t	0.5	2.0	0.6	30	2	1.4	65	3.7	18.5
Chemical fertiliser m. t	0.45	1.3	0.31	23	0.35–0.4	0.52	114	–7.2	10.9
Steel m. t	0.04	0.3	0.06	20	na	0.05*	na	8.4	–4.4
Cloth m. m²	146.4	450.0	175.3	39	380–400	367.1	96	3.7	15.9
Paper 000 t	41.7	130.0	46.8	36	90–100	69.5*	77	2.3	10.4

Sources So Lieu Thong Ke 1930–84, pp. 40, 44–5, 78, 85, 87, 119; Communist Party of Vietnam, *4th National Congress Documents* (Hanoi: FLPH, 1977) p. 64; Pham Van Dong, 'Report to VCP Congress', JPRS, 81345, *Vietnam Report*, no. 2380, pp. 37, 39, 41, 43–6.

avoid the political cycle of existing socialist systems. It is the very real political tensions lying behind this debate which make the process of change very difficult and protracted.

In 1982, after considerable criticism of the 1976–80 plan and its over-ambitious goals, more realistic targets were set with the result that many more products came within reasonable reach of their 1985 targets (Table 6.10). Priorities within the plan were clearly changed from 1976 to 1982. Since then the process of reordering priorities has been extended by the 1986 Party Congress. Table 6.11 sets out clearly the shift in emphasis to the major objectives of the three plans: particularly the rising importance accorded to exports as an economic necessity rather than an aspect of international cooperation; the changing attitude towards heavy industry from one of building 'many new bases' to one of greater realism; and modification of the socialisation objective. In fact by 1986 the artificiality of collectivisation in the South had created a victory for those within the Party who argued for a much more gradualist approach, one in which development of social relations accorded with the need for economic viability of enterprises. If this meant continuation of private enterprise in many areas, so be it. All enterprises will be put to the test of proving their capability of providing incomes according to work.[52]

The 'heavy industry first' strategy was abandoned reluctantly, and the alternatives of 'agriculture-led growth' or a concentration of industrial effort in the labour-intensive, export-orientated growth favoured by some Western theorists have never been wholly embraced. Rather the compromises reached involved time horizons and the relative importance of short-term adjustments to overcome the crisis of disproportionality. Development of heavy industry was to be linked to the immediate needs and capacity of the Vietnamese economy. Le Duan re-stated this in his address to the Sixth Plenum of the Party Central Committee, held in July 1984:[53]

> Priority must be given to the development of *heavy industry*. Only by so doing, can we fulfil the pivotal task of the transitional period: to carry out socialist industrialisation in order to create what we lack most and need most in successfully building socialism and firmly defending the homeland, i.e., a great engineering industry capable of furnishing the whole economy with modern technology, accelerating the formation and consolidation of the socialist rapports [*sic*] of production ... However, preferential development of heavy industry must be rationally carried out at each stage in which efforts should be

Table 6.11 Comparison of economic objectives of Second, Third and Fourth Five Year Plans

Second Five Year Plan (1976–80)	Third Five Year Plan (1981–85)	Fourth Five Year Plan (1986–90)
(1) '... to achieve a sudden spurt of agriculture, to step up forestry and fisheries; vigorously develop light industry and food industry (including handicrafts and small industries) with the aim of catering for the needs of the whole country in food, foodstuffs and an important part of the common consumer goods ...'	(1) 'Resolve the most urgent problems in order to stabilise and improve step by step the people's conditions of life ...'	(1) '... the three major programs for grain and feed products consumer and export goods ... are not only of vital significance to the immediate situation, but also the primary, essential conditions for proceeding with socialist industrialisation in the subsequent stage.'
(2) '... turn to full account the existing heavy industry capacity and build many new bases of heavy industry, especially the engineering industry, in order to serve agriculture, forestry, fishery and light industry first of all ... actively expand communications transport; rapidly increase the capacity of capital construction; promote scientific and technological work ...'	(2) 'Develop and reorganise production ... concentrate efforts on agriculture ... supply more electricity, coal, mechanical products, metals, chemical products, raw materials to the economic base units and distribute them in a concentrated manner, according to a rational ordering of priorities, on the basis of detailed calculation of economic returns ... proceed towards redeployment of the work force ... consolidate existing new economic zones ...'	(2) '... develop a number of heavy industrial sectors and infrastructures that are necessary for and suitable to our capabilities in the immediate future. These are energy, some engineering establishments, raw and other materials, communications and transport, postal communications ...'
	(3) 'Reorganise basic construction according to	(3) '... reducing the rate of inflation and narrowing the gap of imbalance between goods and currencies ... eliminating inappropriate regulations on the transport

and sale of goods in order to increase the volume of goods rapidly ...'

(4) '... closely combine social sciences, natural sciences and science and technology to develop a strategy for socio-economic development ... In particular ... to serve the three major programs ...'

(5) '... renovation of the people's life ... solve social problems from employment to material and cultural life ...'

(6) 'Adjustment of guidelines for and structure of investment ... the problem is not only to create sources of capital. What is equally important is how to use and manage these sources in the most effective manner.'

our capacities and in a way which exploits existing material and technical bases ...'

(4) 'Perfect the work of distribution and circulation of products ... Readjust the system of prices by sure steps, make resolute efforts to control then stabilise prices. Assure the purchasing power of real wages of workers, cadres and civil servants.'

(5) 'Push socialist transformation resolutely; achieve, in essentials, agricultural cooperation in the Nam Bo provinces with production collectives as the general form ...'

(6) 'Assure good economic cooperation with the Soviet Union, Laos and Cambodia, as well as with CMEA countries ...'

(3) 'Use all the social work force; organise and manage the labour force well in order to achieve a marked increase in social labour productivity ...'

(4) 'Achieve basic socialist transformation in the South ...'

(5) 'Rapidly increase the sources of export products, first of all agricultural and light industry products ...'

(6) 'Strive to develop education, culture and health work ...'

(7) 'Effect a deep change in economic organisation and management ...'

Continued on page 194.

Table 6.11 Comparison of economic objectives of Second, Third and Fourth Five Year Plans (*continued*)

Second Five Year Plan (1976–80)	Third Five Year Plan (1981–85)	Fourth Five Year Plan (1986–90)
	(7) 'Practise strict thrift, especially in basic construction and production . . .' (8) '. . . a great and rapid application of scientific knowledge and technical progress . . .' (9) 'Renovate the system of economic management . . .'	(7) 'Renovate the planning mechanism . . . use efficiently the various policies of economic levers.'

Sources Communist Party of Vietnam, *Fourth National Congress Documents* (Hanoi: FLPH, 1977) pp. 63–4; Parti Communiste du Vietnam, *Ve Congrès National Rapport Politique* (Hanoi: FLPH, 1982), pp. 81–7; Vo Van Kiet 'Economic Report' to the Sixth Party Congress, *SWB*, FE/8449 23 December 1986.

focused in selected branches of heavy industry and, on the basis of the development of agriculture and light industry, proper scale and degree of heavy industry's development should be defined. At the initial stage, primary attention must be given to the development of agriculture and light industry, whence heavy industry can procure sources of capital, labour, food and foodstuffs for workers, equipment and materials for factories, and markets for its products ... Nevertheless, each progress of agriculture and light industry is made under the impact of heavy industry, and aims to strengthen the basis of the development of heavy industry.

In the relationship between heavy industry, on the one hand, and agriculture and light industry, on the other, the role of the former as rational priority and that of the latter as basis create conditions for each other's development, and such a structural connection is a law of economic development.

What appears in this rather convoluted passage is not merely a juggling act. It is an admission that heavy industry growth is needed to overcome bottlenecks and shortages in consuming industries rather than being the 'leading link' sector, outstripping all other sectors and bringing the rest of the economy along in its wake. Despite the need to accelerate growth of agriculture and light industry expressed in the above quotation, there is also recognition that heavy industry should continue to be developed, not because of Party desires to bring forward the future, but as part of a medium-term response to an unbalanced structure of production.

The continued emphasis on development of the producer goods industries under the Second Five Year Plan is borne out by data on the distribution of state investment in Table 6.12. In spite of the renewed stress on regional rather than centrally managed industries, on consumer goods rather than the heavy industries, and towards agricultural development in order to shore up the standard of living of the population, this table shows an apparently paradoxical result. After the reforms, state investment in agriculture was a smaller proportion of the total than in 1976–9 and industry's share was correspondingly higher. Within industry, the share of the producer goods branch also rose after 1980 compared with the consumer goods branch; that of central level industries increased from just over 60 per cent in the earlier period to over 70 per cent in the later one.

These figures do not, however, necessarily reflect the actual investment situation. By 1987, about 15 per cent of investment was carried

Table 6.12 Structure of State investment outlays 1975–84, per cent

Year	All Sectors Agri-culture	Industry All	A	B	Industry Group A	Group B	Central	Local
1975	13.9	–	–	–	–	–	64.8	35.2
1976	20.0	31.9	21.4	10.5	67.1	32.9	62.7	37.3
1977	26.3	31.5	24.0	7.5	76.2	23.8	62.5	37.5
1978	24.0	32.2	22.2	10.0	68.9	31.1	59.0	41.0
1979	23.8	35.9	25.9	10.0	72.1	27.9	67.0	33.0
1980	19.0	40.7	29.3*	11.3*	72.1*	27.9*	73.6	26.4
1981	26.7	41.7	35.0	6.7	83.9	16.1	73.7	26.3
1982	15.7	53.2	45.3	7.9	85.2	14.8	75.2	24.8
1983	16.7	40.4	n/a	n/a	n/a	n/a	71.3	28.7
1984	24.2	36.0	n/a	n/a	n/a	n/a	71.1	28.9

*Estimate based on revised data.
Source *So Lieu Thong Ke, 1979*, pp. 39, 41, 44; *1982*, pp. 39, 41, 44;
1930–84, pp. 75–6.

out independently by local authorities and by state, collective and private enterprises under the economic reforms.[54] We cannot say at present how this investment effort is distributed.

Priorities of state investment within industry sectors have also been modified in order to concentrate the State's investment effort in some key areas – to increase investment in industries providing necessary inputs to agriculture, for example, and to overcome major bottlenecks which have slowed down the growth of production and led to severe under-utilisation of capacity. According to one official I spoke to in Hanoi, no less than 30 per cent of industrial investment in 1984 went to construction of electric power generating capacity; this probably accounts for two-fifths of the investment in Group A for that year.

The energy industry is clearly a 'heavy industry', but it is also important to remember that Group A (or the producer goods sector) contains industries which are by no means 'heavy' – ranging from those producing traditional farm implements to parts of the electronics industry. The tendency of Vietnamese leaders to conflate 'heavy industry' with the producer goods sector in their speeches is therefore quite misleading. In the absence of further data on allocation of investment funds by branch of industry, it is impossible to say whether this shift towards Group A is in fact a shift towards 'heavy industry', or whether it disguises some movement towards development of light engineering. But it is worth noting that in two branches of the producer goods sector (machining and chemicals), there has been a considerable shift in *output* share towards the small industry and handicraft sector, since 1975.[55]

Figures on the overall rate of investment out of national income are not published, but we do know that state investment grew more rapidly during 1976–80 than national income. During the next two years investment in construction remained more or less stable, while investment in new capital equipment fell by about a third, so that the sharp rise in the share of Group A shown in the table is out of a smaller total investment. The fall in total investment was accompanied by a growth in real national income of over 12 per cent in these two years, so clearly there was a drop in the rate of investment. The combination of falling investment and growth in national income also points to increased effectiveness of investment. In 1983 and 1984, however, investment rose again much more rapidly than the growth in national income.[56] A further attempt to raise the effectiveness of investment was seen in the effort to halt the rapid growth of new projects in the annual plan for 1986, which aimed to keep investment levels down to those of 1983.[57] At the Sixth Party Congress in late 1986, a by now strongly reform-minded leadership emphasised previous laxity in allowing new large-scale projects to go ahead; and 'bureaucratic centralism', as major causes of continued economic inefficiencies.[58]

Apart from improved effectiveness of investment, pressure on per capita consumption, which had built up in the 1970s, could be relieved by outside injections of capital. The foreign aid contribution to the Vietnamese investment effort in the post-war period has been substantial. Since the termination of Chinese assistance in 1978, the CMEA countries have provided investment for heavy industry, releasing local accumulation for investment in consumer goods, light engineering and agriculture (although CMEA aid has also been important in developing processed agricultural exports). According to the then vice-premier in charge of economic affairs, Tran Phuong, Soviet economic aid during the Second Five Year Plan amounted to the equivalent of $US 1.45 billion. After 1981, the amounts were apparently reduced with grant aid only 'a few tens of millions of dollars' and the majority of aid in the form of 20–30-year loans (at not more than two per cent p.a. interest).[59] CMEA-built industries in 1984 accounted for 100 per cent of production in tin, sulphuric acid, superphosphate and coffee, 82 per cent of metal-working machine tools, 89 per cent of coal and 35 per cent of electric power generation.[60] In addition, Soviet assistance has been responsible for the establishment of cement, housing construction materials, concrete railway sleepers, battery plants, rubber, cotton and tea plantations and processing facilities, oil exploration and completion of the Thang Long bridge over the Red River. Scandinavian aid has been important in some other large projects notably in paper and cement.

Because it is the main source of aid to finance imports, the Soviet Union is also Vietnam's most important trading partner: between 1981 and 1984, it supplied 7.1 million tonnes of oil and oil products, 3.4 million tonnes of nitrogenous fertiliser, 12 640 trucks, as well as large quantities of raw cotton, ferrous metal and 0.72 million tonnes of grain.[61] It would appear that, as under the DRV, Vietnamese imports from the USSR are heavily concentrated in producer goods. But consumer goods are also involved. In mid-1985, Ho Chi Minh City signed a contract with the USSR to export wickerwork, liquor, embroidery, sporting gear, palm-leaf articles, plastic goods, dried and canned fruit and farm produce in exchange for aluminium utensils, detergents, refrigerators, irons, watches and film.[62] Improvement in the growth rate of the Vietnamese economy, most particularly in its ability to export, has, however, meant a shift towards trade with the West since the early 1980s. Exports to the convertible currency area have grown more rapidly than to CMEA, and there has been a marked improvement in Vietnam's ability to pay for imports from the West by exporting. Such imports are primarily capital and intermediate goods while exports are generally unprocessed agricultural or marine products and handicraft manufactures.[63]

Availability of foreign aid has enabled the maintenance of levels of investment in heavy industry projects well beyond what could have been achieved, given the severe consumption constraint based on domestic accumulation. There are also some indications, as noted above, that the rate of investment has not been allowed to rise so that in spite of an apparent shift in emphasis towards Group A and the centrally run industries, there have been improvements in its structural allocation and effectiveness. It is also clear that there has been a reverse movement in the composition of output since 1979 (Tables 6.13 and 6.14), particularly towards regionally operated industries. And while all industry has grown more rapidly since 1979, the consumer goods sector (Group B) has grown faster than producer goods. A good deal of this development in the consumer goods and light industries and in locally managed sectors has occurred in the South – fuelled by agricultural growth following introduction of the product contract system and price reform and in turn providing further incentives for increased agricul-

Table 6.13 Structure of industry: shares of gross output 1975–84, per cent

Year	Group A	Group B	Handi-craft	Modern industry	Central	Local
1975	37.8	62.2	37.8	62.2	43.6	56.4
1976	38.6	61.4	–	–	44.9	55.1
1977	35.2	64.8	–	–	45.4	54.6
1978	37.2	62.8	–	–	46.0	54.0
1979	36.4	63.6	–	–	41.5	58.5
1980	40.3	59.7	43.4	56.6	38.6	61.4
1981	43.1	56.9	–	–	38.6	61.4
1982	39.3	60.7	–	–	35.1	64.9
1983	34.9	65.1	42.8	57.2	37.4	62.6
1984	34.5	65.5	40.0	60.0	36.8	63.2

Source *So Lieu Thong Ke,* 1979, p. 29; 1982, p. 29; 1985, p. 42.

Table 6.14 Growth-rates of industrial sectors (1970 constant prices), per cent

Period	Group A	Group B	Handi-craft	Modern industry	Central	Local	Total
1975–82	5.7	7.8	–	–	2.6	9.8	7.0
1975–79	4.7	6.3	5.3†	0.5†	4.4	6.7	5.7
1979–82	7.2	9.8	–	–	0.2	14.2	8.9
1982–84*	9.0	12.3	7.6§	7.0§	11.2	11.0	11.1

*1982 constant prices; †1975–80; §1983–84.
Source *So Lieu Thong Ke, 1930–84*, pp. 40–2.

tural output. The greater volume and quality of consumer goods available in the South since 1980 has been observed by many visitors, although statistical evidence is harder to come by. A few figures can be found however: in Ho Chi Minh City, the value of industrial output was reported to have risen by over 26 per cent in 1980–1 and 1983–4 consumer goods production is by far the largest sector in the city, though light engineering has increased its share from 8.3 per cent in 1976 to 20 per cent in 1984.[64] Ho Chi Minh City now accounts for about 30 per cent of industrial production in the country, so the fast rate of growth accounts for a rather high proportion of the total growth in consumer goods output. Similarly, in Cuu Long province, where consumer goods and some small machinery workshops account for most of the output, the real value of industrial production (1982 prices) is reported to have risen by an average of 26 per cent per annum between 1981 and 1984 (compared with 11 per cent p.a. in 1976–80).[65]

Another sign of more effective use of investment, a better structure of production and improved incentives can be seen in the indications that productivity of labour in industry has begun to rise, after a period of stagnation (Table 6.15). The available measures of labour productivity are rather crude: it is not possible, for example, to obtain a measure of real product per man-hour on the basis of published data. However, the figures do suggest that after rising from 1975 to 1978, average labour productivity fell sharply in 1979–80 and recovered thereafter. Marginal labour productivity (extra output per additional labourer) rose over the period – averaging 6.4 thousand dong per additional worker in 1975–9 and 26.8 thousand dong in 1979–82 (both figures in 1970 constant prices).

Some indication is also available of average labour productivity in the small industry and handicrafts branch. In 1975 output per worker in this branch was only 50 per cent of that in industry as a whole. By 1984 the figure had risen to 62 per cent.[66] In other words, productivity rose faster in the handicraft sector than in modern industry.

But while Le Duan's Sixth Plenum speech cited above pays careful attention to the problem of proportionality in development, emphasising the importance of increasing supplies of manufactured consumer

Table 6.15 Labour productivity in industry and handicrafts

Year	Industrial workforce 000s	Gross value of output m. dong	Output per worker dong	Index (1982 = 100)
1975	1 890.2	7 288.4	3 856	76
1976	2 033.4	8 208.9	4 037	79
1977	2 165.6	9 028.9	4 169	82
1978	2 185.3	9 520.1	4 356	85
1979	2 237.8	9 089.9	4 062	80
1980	2 235.6	8 218.4	3 676	72
1981	2 273.2	9 463.0	4 163	82
1982	2 300.7	11 724.4	5 096	100
1982	2 300.7	72 095.8	31 336	100
1983	2 223.1	82 999.8	37 335	119
1984	2 301.3	88 995.2	38 672	123

Note Values for 1975–82 are in 1970 constant prices; values for 1982–84 are in 1982 constant prices.
Sources *So Lieu Thong Ke, 1979*, p. 28; *1982*, p. 28; *1930–84*, pp. 63, 68.

goods in boosting peasant production as well as the role of modern inputs, it is clear that there are continuing tensions between this approach (what Kornai has referred to as 'harmonic' growth strategy) and the more ambitious 'rush' to build new heavy industrial plants which was characteristic of the Second Five Year Plan. Only a page after the above passage Le Duan continued:

> We must always take the initiative and take advantage of all opportunities and capabilities to embark on the construction of a number of key heavy-industry projects especially engineering and metallurgy projects. There will be neither heavy industry nor socialism without steel and engineering.[67]

The mention of steel at this point is interesting both because it has not generally been mentioned as a priority area during either the Second Five Year Plan or the 1986–90 period[68] and because in many ways the steel industry has epitomised the problems plaguing Vietnamese industrial development since 1965.

The construction of a major steelworks at Thai Nguyen in North Vietnam was an early priority of the Vietnamese leadership and the First Five Year Plan (1961–5) stipulated an output goal of 200 000 tonnes of iron and steel per annum. In fact in its one year of operation prior to the damage caused by US bombing, it produced 127 800 tonnes of pig iron.[69] Owing to the lack of development of Vietnamese iron ore deposits and the unsuitability of Vietnam's high quality anthracite for coking, most of the raw materials for the plant were imported from China and its output was exported to China.[70] The plant has never reached its original design capacity. Restoration work was begun in the mid-1970s and planned output by 1980 was 300 000 tonnes of steel, but actual output in that year was reported at 62 300 tonnes. In 1984–5, annual steel output was even lower.[71]

The difficulties since 1975 can be partly assigned to the break in relations with China. But as Rawski has pointed out in relation to the early development of China's own steel industry, the advanced technology involved in steel-making and narrow tolerances required for making good quality steel, are often beyond the experience and skills of a workforce which is new to industry and, perhaps more relevant to present day Vietnam, may overstrain the existing infrastructure, causing delays in production. The alternatives may be to cut production (with resulting losses in economies of scale) or sacrifice quality which will produce additional costs elsewhere in the economy.[72] Problems of this sort can also be seen in Vietnam at the Vinh Phu paper mill, constructed with Swedish assistance during the Second Five Year Plan. This mill, which incorporates advanced technology, has suffered from numerous teething problems including shortage of skilled workers and severe difficulties in obtaining raw materials, although production is now increasing. One further problem in building this type of large-scale, high technology plant in a country like Vietnam is that aside from the normal gestation period, the sorts of problem described above can mean that by the time the plant becomes fully operational, it may no longer represent the best technology: it may have achieved what Kalecki called 'moral obsolescence'.

Rawski contrasts the experience of steel with that of China's machinery industry where relatively low capital intensity and the possibility of considerable technical advances through 'learning by doing' made the transition from carrying out repairs on imported machinery to the production of spare parts and then complete machines easier. Those areas of China's producer goods industries which had been relatively long-established and had an experienced and skilled workforce were able to continue after 1949 to generate techno-logical progress, producing progressively higher quality products and increasing output, although they received few state investment re-sources compared with newly industrialising regions.

The problem then, is not with producer goods industries as such, but in choosing the wrong 'leading link' (that is, one having few inter-sectoral linkages with the rest of the economy) and in choosing to develop industries which overtax the existing resource base of the economy. In Vietnam the tendency still exists, among some political leaders, to push for the development of productive forces by raising the rate of investment out of national income and concentrating on the development of a wide range of producer goods industries which would give the country an independent technological capability. This 'rush' approach inevitably creates barriers to further growth by generating crises of 'underproduction', by creating new demands (for wage goods and raw materials) which cannot be satisfied. And in Vietnam these shortages were exacerbated by the difficulties of the post-war readjust-ment and continuing military mobilisation.[73]

Perhaps the most trenchant criticism of this tendency, as well as the proof of its continuing strength, came from an article by Planning Minister Vo Van Kiet in October 1985. Having said that the improve-ments in planning in the 1980s 'still look like patchwork' and were 'mostly on paper', Kiet continued:

We can cite the major shortcomings in planning work that exist, not in the past, but today. Plans are unrealistic and originate from subjective requirements ... The biggest imbalance – which is seldom analysed when assessing a planning period – is that between our subjective desires and our actual capabilities. Proceeding from this wistful starting point, planning work has been carried out in accordance with a series of criteria imposed by higher echelons as well as with a series of directives and regulations, all having the effect of law, that are not consistent with the various policies and economic incentives ... Faced with the choice between producing wealth but violating regulations and probably courting much trouble in the process and continuing to sustain failures and losses but being left alone and even earning praise, basic units must go for the second option ... although we speak of doing planning work from the lower level, the higher level continues, with all their 'justifiable' arguments, to apply pressure for the purpose of ensuring at all cost the fulfilment of the norms set by the upper echelons ... The upper echelons, in the name of the entire cause, set very rigorous requirements, but often fail to provide sufficient material conditions for the basic units to carry out their plans. Being inherently imbalanced [*sic*] with the prescribed tasks, supplies are often 'diverted' to other unplanned purposes.[74]

Renewed growth, on the other hand, has depended very largely on the ability to develop more realistic plans and on the concomitant introduction of incentive systems and other economic levers to improve effectiveness in the use of resources at the microeconomic level.

REFORMING THE MANAGEMENT SYSTEM

The changes already made in the planned allocation system, taking account of the actual resources available to firms, were the first step towards improved performance of the economy. However, the effectiveness of investment in productive capacity cannot be ensured without simultaneously getting rid of economic signals which lead firms and workers to act contrary to the intentions of planners. An important ingredient of the sluggish performance of Vietnamese industry in the past has, according to Vo Van Kiet, been the existence of a 'bureaucratic centralism and subsidisation system' (also referred to as 'administrative planning methods') at all levels of economic management – a system which produces conflicts of interest between the planning authorities and the production units.

Kiet attacked the tendency, under the system of planning which had emerged in Vietnam during the war, for higher authorities to try to plan every aspect of economic life. This, he said had the effect of making enterprises and workers dependent upon decisions from above, unable to make changes in order to meet rapidly changing conditions. A major cause of demoralisation and low productivity in industry was the coexistence of 'responsibility' at lower levels with lack of effective control:

> By issuing orders, higher-level agencies usually avoid responsibility for setbacks. All setbacks and their consequences are shouldered by the primary installations. Never has an order-issuing agency been punished for issuing a wrong order or for taking time to fulfil the urgent demands of lower echelons, no matter how much damage this may cause. However, there are many types of punishment for production installations. For example, if higher echelons assign plan norms without securing the necessary conditions for implementing them or if they set forth incorrect prices, those who comply suffer losses while the higher echelon agencies are not held responsible for anything. This leads to the practice of deliberately issuing orders in order to avoid responsibility.[75]

This criticism echoes earlier comments about the effects of the failure to assign real authority to base units.[76] Another outspoken criticism by a district-level Party official in 1981, for example, asked how it was possible for district authorities to function as planners when they were allowed no control over supplies of key inputs and capital and no important sources of revenue.[77] A major aspect of the move to revitalise economic management and improve the productivity of industry was therefore, in the view of the reformers, to increase the level of financial independence of production installations.

The process of decentralising economic decision-making began in a small way following the Sixth Plenum decisions in August 1979. While the main focus of these reforms remained on promotion of agricultural production, some measures were introduced to allow greater autonomy of planning by locally-managed industries and to allow direct trade between enterprises in goods not covered by the central plan. Firms using imported raw materials were also permitted to establish direct contact with foreign suppliers. Goods not purchased by the State, could be sold directly to consumers.

Since 1979, foreign trade has been decentralised, with provinces, cities and even districts having their own import–export branches which are intended to act as clearing houses for exporting and importing enterprises. Large-volume exporters are now permitted to deal directly with customers. Exporting enterprises receive a quarter of their foreign exchange earnings in the form of imported goods. At the Sixth Party Congress the intention to link access to imported goods even more closely to the export performance of enterprises was announced. However, Vietnamese leaders are very resistant to the idea of enterprises competing with each other in local and foreign markets, rejecting an important stimulus to reduced local self-sufficiency and improved productivity and quality in some areas. There are also pressures to reduce the level of luxury consumer goods import which has emerged under this system, notably in the South. Increased retention of profits by firms for internal accumulation and bonus funds has also been introduced in an effort to give greater flexibility in responding to changes in supply and demand conditions as well as enable the provision of more adequate production incentives to workers.

The system of direct trading between enterprises has also been extended to include goods within the state plan, in order to cut down on the number of intermediary organisations involved in domestic circulation of goods. Whereas in 1979 it was reported that in order to transport umbrella stands from Tay Ninh to Saigon, the production unit had to 'go through 17 agencies, obtain 15 seals, sign 5 contracts and pay many different types of tax',[78] the measures introduced by mid-1985 included provisions to allow large consumers of coal, for example, to obtain it directly from the mine while smaller consumers need only go through one intermediary link. Large retail stores were also permitted to buy direct from the producer, according to the distribution plans assigned to them, instead of from state intermediate trading organisations.[79] These measures are particularly aimed at cutting delivery delays which have persistently disrupted production in the past and at reducing opportunities for favouritism and corruption in the allocation of goods. By enabling firms to extend their market activities beyond administrative boundaries, they are also an important step in breaking down local autarky.

Decentralisation of economic decision-making represents a fundamental shift in the operation of the economic system in Vietnam.

Instead of directly interfering in the production and investment activities of enterprises, the role of the state planning authorities is now seen as 'to create conditions for economic establishments to operate effectively'.[80] Central control is to be exercised by means of 'laws and economic policies and the policy on technological advances', setting limits beyond which enterprises cannot go rather than by direct administrative control. Since 1979 the number of products subjected to legally-binding plans has steadily diminished, until in 1987 this was confined to those considered 'really necessary to ensure basic balances and the commitments to foreign countries',[81] In all other cases the use of economic levers to achieve targets is authorised.

The decentralisation policies are associated with changed thinking about the development of socialist production relations. Although lip service was paid to the notion that collectivisation should be voluntary and based on economic benefits to those concerned, in practice as we have seen, more emphasis was placed on changing ownership structures as such, than on creating economically viable institutions which would generate higher incomes and avoid conflicts of interest between co-operators and the State. The 1986 victory of the economic reformers in the Party has led to a clear revision of this practice. The political report to the Sixth Congress warned against pursuing harassment or discrimination against individuals not willing to join collectives, arguing that some areas of the economy could not yet be profitably transformed into collective ownership. Neither organisation and management skills, nor social infrastructure are sufficiently well developed for this to be successful. While economic policies (on investment, taxation and credit) will be structured to provide advantages for the collective sector, the report argues that equality before the law must be observed:

> Those who turn out material wealth and render useful services to society, fulfil their obligations, abide by the law and policies, are respected and entitled to enjoy incomes corresponding to the results of their legal labour and undertakings. Lazy and parasitic elements should be criticised and forced to work ... That is the consistent policy towards all citizens, regardless of the economic sectors they belong to.[82]

Though it will have something of a headstart on the private sector, then, the state and collective sector will nevertheless be forced to compete with the private sector if its hoped-for economic superiority is to emerge. As the 1986 political report observed, it had proved impossible to abolish the private sector by 'wishful thinking'.[83] Giving the socialist sector a chance to be competitive has therefore been the prime rationale behind the adoption of decentralisation policies.

An important example used to encourage widespread adoption of this approach has been the success of the Ho Chi Minh City Food Corporation, a State-run purchasing authority which successfully ignored official prices and crossed administrative trade boundaries for four years before being given official approval for its practices by the central Government. During this period of illegal operations, the company was protected by the leading southern Party officials who now dominate economic policy-making in Hanoi. As the company's volume of trade increased, it was able to control food prices in the city and bring private food traders into its orbit, ultimately making them company agents and enabling a reduction in size of the city's food administration from 4000 employees to 30. Since 1983 the company has branched out into food processing, sometimes in joint ventures with other firms, and has established an oil refinery (despite objections from the Energy Ministry) to secure supplies of fuel for its manufacturing activities. The projects have been financed by borrowing from overseas Vietnamese (who have also provided technical advice) and by the company's own foreign exchange earnings.[84] In early 1988, the company's director, Mme Nguyen Thi Thi, also became a director of a new State-owned bank in Ho Chi Minh City which offers competitive interest rates to depositors.

An implication of decentralised financial authority and competition is that firms must be allowed to go bankrupt. While this is not explicitly broached in the major policy statements (for example, of the Sixth Party Congress), it is nevertheless a key element in ensuring that the new policies will work. Under the administrative planning system, lack of effective financial responsibility of managers, combined with acute shortages, has led many state enterprises to have low capacity utilisation, high cost structures and to depend upon state subsidies for their continued operation. This in turn has been a major contributing factor in state budget deficits and high rates of inflation prevailing in the economy. To increase the circulation of commodities and reduce the rate of inflation it is therefore necessary to eliminate these subsidies and the enormous waste of resources which goes with the shortage economy. Firms which prove unable to improve their profitability under the impact of reforms will have to be considered for closure, unless they can be shown to be of national or strategic importance. This will apply to several industries in which the small size of the domestic market prevents economies of scale arising and for which export markets cannot be developed in the medium term due to high production costs and poor quality of products.

The difficulty in implementing such measures are manifold. Whole bureaucracies are established to manage these industries (mostly falling into Group A) and large numbers of workers also face redundancy if factories are closed. The Vietnamese economy already has a rather high rate of unemployment[85] and resistance from workers and bureaucrats alike to factory closures is unlikely to be avoided. Although state salaries are generally very low, there are incentives for workers to remain in the state sector because of the paid sick leave, annual leave, maternity leave, in-service training schemes and other welfare provisions not always available to those in the private and collective sectors. As in the case of the agricultural cooperatives, the possibility of increasing the level of income in the longer run has to be weighed against short-term interests of workers in preserving these cushions against poverty. Vietnamese leaders have acknowledged that their 'greatest problem' is that 'quite a number of sectors and localities have tended to make adjustments reluctantly'[86] and that 'renovation is not only held back by the force of habit, but also runs up against the privilege and prerogatives of some people who stick to the old mechanism'.[87] These strictures are aimed at the bureaucracy in particular, and at those Party cadres whose constituency lies within the bureaucracy and whose political control over economic resources is threatened by financial decentralisation, competitive pressures and reduced economic autarky. However, it may also be possible for these groups to find allies in some sections of the working class. It stands to reason that in the North, where administrative planning has been long established, the reform will be more difficult to implement than in the South.

A second major area of reform aimed at improving the production effectiveness of industrial enterprises has been in the system of remuneration. Complaints have been centred on both the level of wages and on the structure of wage differentials, and reform is essential if workers are to perceive clear benefits to themselves from the new management system.

As a result of the acute shortages of food and other consumer goods and rising free market prices, remuneration of urban workers has generally been acknowledged to be below subsistence levels since the late 1970s. One report given to the Fifth Party Congress in 1982 argued that present wage and bonus policies did not insure that the energy expended in labour is replenished ... due to unreasonable policies regulating income, the income of manual workers, generally speaking, is lower than the income of all other strata of the population.[88]

Poor health was a direct consequence of inadequate standards of consumption and, the report continued, 'the number of workers retiring early as a result of poor health is rising.' In the handicraft sector there were also reports of cooperatives channelling too much income into accumulation funds, leaving insufficient for distribution according to labour effort.[89] As mentioned above, the low official wages have forced many workers to look for alternative ways of making an income, including illegal use of State property, corruption, private trading, etc., and the higher remuneration available outside the State sector has led to widespread absenteeism, low motivation and low labour productivity in industry.

Some efforts have been made to increase output and workers' incomes by improving the system of individual incentives. In some industries, it would appear that wage differentials hardly existed at all prior to the introduction of reforms. Of the 75 000 workers belonging to the central light industrial sector in 1978, for example, 88 per cent were reportedly at the same wage level.[90] In an attempt to relate workers' income more directly to labour expended, piece-rates began to be applied in 1980, beginning at the Pho Yen Ball-Bearing factory and the Internal Combustion Engine Spare Parts Factory No. 2 in Bien Hoa with additional bonuses and penalties applied according to quality of product and efficient consumption of raw materials.[91] By 1982 the system had evidently spread to only nineteen factories and, given the rather low technological level of many aspects of Vietnamese industry, this is somewhat surprising. One of the reasons for the slowness in adoption of the piece-rate system may be that if involved reorganisation of the labour process away from job specialisation to product-based collectives. But a more fundamental reason has been the inability of piece-rates to solve the problem of continuing shortages of food and basic consumer goods.[92] By 1982, Haiphong waterside workers on piece-rates, were earning almost twice the income of time-rated vehicle repairmen at the docks, but in neither case were their wages sufficient to meet the minimum subsistence requirements of the workers and their dependents.[93]

The key to improving workers' living standards lies in a fundamental revision of the price system as a whole (including wages). This has been part of a drive to make the concept of 'economic accounting' (the Soviet system of *khozraschet*) a reality. During the war, the over-riding emphasis in pricing policy was on stability and this meant that important changes in costs of production, brought about by the bombing and ensuing shortages, tended to be ignored. One of the major problems facing industrial firms in Vietnam has been that because of the inability of the State to supply adequate raw materials, firms have been forced to turn to the free market, to obtain supplies and meet production plans. This has led to a situation where many firms operated continually at a loss and has been a major reason for the existence of widespread subsidies. Other reasons for the persistence of subsidies have included the tendency to over-ordering, under-utilisation of capacity and waste of resources induced by the shortages and 'rush' growth strategies. Moreover, the state-subsidised food ration paid to workers has been a factor keeping wages low, leading to over-manning of factories combined with low productivity. Consumption subsidies have in fact been the largest single item in the State budget, taking twelve per cent of expenditure in 1983,[94] and making a major contribution to inflationary budget deficits.

The first attempt to revise the price structure came in late 1981 when official food procurement prices were revised upwards, with even larger increases in prices of agricultural inputs (see Chapter 4). While this did improve the relationship of many prices to actual supply and demand conditions, a serious side effect was to increase the gap between official procurement prices and the subsidised ration price, with a concomitant impact on the budget deficit. An attempt to rectify this situation came after the Eighth Central Committee Plenum in August 1985 when it was announced that the food subsidy would be abolished and all wages would henceforth be paid in cash. Large wage increases – often to as much as 15 times the old level – for State employees were awarded to compensate for the price change.

This reform was never given a chance to work as almost simultaneously the State Bank implemented a currency reform, replacing ten old dong with one new one. The aim here was to reduce private accumulations of wealth by limiting the amount of currency which could be converted. Its impact was disastrous. As we have already seen, the economy as a whole depended to a significant extent on transactions in the free market for its day-to-day functioning. For State enterprises, this meant holding cash reserves in hand instead of handing revenues immediately over to the State Bank as demanded by law. The value of these cash reserves was slashed by the currency reform as was the working capital of private enterprises and the result was a drastic increase in the shortages of goods in urban markets and an inflationary surge in prices. The impact was worsened by panic buying and the subsidised food ration had to be restored when inflation reached such proportions that workers could no longer make ends meet on their new higher wages. The impact on prices had been too great to control easily and the inflation rate reportedly rose from 50 per cent per annum before the currency reform to 1000 per cent in 1986–7.[95]

Price reform continues to be a major priority of the Government, the main elements of policy being to stabilise prices by deregulation of the market – removing barriers to trade which encourage hoarding and speculation by private traders on the one hand, and a retreat into autarky by peasants, on the other – and gradually introducing a single price system, eliminating multi-tiered prices for goods and multiple exchange rates in foreign transactions. The experience of other socialist countries has shown that price reform is inevitably accompanied by some inflation, precisely because the use of queuing and rationing to deal with shortages is a form of suppressed inflation. One lesson from the Vietnamese experience of 1985 is that price reform cannot be undertaken in the absence of other measures to stimulate an increase in the supply of goods.[96] It therefore needs to be a gradual process, linked to the rate of change in output which in turn depends upon the investment strategy being pursued. The difficulty for countries like Vietnam in carrying out a process of reform stems from both the long-term nature of carrying out adjustments to the industrial structure to achieve a better input-output balance and political resistance to attempts to wind down large-scale, but low productivity and loss making projects.

For South Vietnam these problems are less intractable than for the North with its large legacy of administrative planning and 'heavy industry first'. The industrial structure of the North remains dominated by large capital goods producing enterprises and the fetters they place on growth in other areas. Shortages of basic inputs like fertiliser and electricity as well as consumer goods continue to hamper the growth of North Vietnamese agricultural output.[97] An increase in imported supplies is hindered by lack of marketable surpluses for export. Thus the self-reinforcing nature of continuing 'goods famine' and low marketed agricultural surpluses has lessened the impact of management reforms on the rate of growth in the region.

The main goal of reform in the system of economic management has been to replace the system of direct administrative control by the use of economic incentives – to make the economic interests of individuals and enterprise managements consistent with the fulfilment of plan targets. These are determined at a wider social level – not by a system of material balances drawn up by planners, but chiefly through the political process whereby economic policies are used to pull rather than push the economy in the desired direction. At the time of writing there is still a certain amount of confusion surrounding the implementation of these reforms. In the words of Vo Van Kiet:

> ... even with our determination to abolish the mechanism of bureaucratic centralism and the system of subsidisation, our policies still cannot develop their results rapidly. The struggle for dominance among different concepts for socio-economic management may take place and differences may persist. A 'chaotic' situation is a reality that is hard to avoid, especially at a time when we have yet to renovate uniformly and thoroughly the mechanism and to arrange the machinery and personnel for developing and employing this mechanism ... In a way, planning has not only failed to contribute toward accelerating the renovation of the general mechanism, but it has also created restrictions and obstacles that hinder the renovation process and even oppose the requirements for renovation.[98]

In spite of the improved performance of the 1980s, then, growth remains unsteady. Given the rather high population growth rate and low standard of living, planners have very little margin of safety in devising the combinations of incentives which could achieve the correct balances between investment and consumption expenditure, between investment in different sectors and between competing political pressures.

7 Socialist Commodity Production

> As it is the power of exchanging that gives occasion to the division of
> labour, so the extent of this division must always be limited by the
> extent of that power, or, in other words, by the extent of the market.
>
> Adam Smith, *Wealth of Nations*

In the introduction to this book an approach to the analysis of markets
in socialist countries like Vietnam was proposed, taking account of the
fact that markets can be looked at on two quite different planes which
bring out more profoundly the implications of exchange and markets
for the structure of society than the more orthodox focus on resource
allocation. On the one hand, the market affects the distribution of
society's resources – this is the problem economists normally address
when they talk about 'plan versus market'. On the other hand, market
forces affect the very organisation and growth of production, the
development of new social relationships through the fundamental
restructuring of society's productive forces.

Economic growth, as Marx pointed out, requires two distinct phases
of production and circulation to take place. In every growing economic
system, regardless of its mode of production, not only must a surplus be
produced and appropriated, but the goods produced must be circulated
among those who will consume them (either as means of production or
as consumer goods). This was expressed by Marx in his discussion of
the 'circulation of capital as a whole' and also in the reproduction
schemes of Volume II of *Capital* which have formed the basis of the
debates on growth discussed in the previous chapter. This analysis
brings out clearly the dual aspect of the growth process. First, there is
the organisation of production itself: the key to this is the way society's
labour force is deployed with the progressive division and re-division
of labour giving rise to increased labour productivity, rapid expansion
of output and accumulation of surpluses. Second is the circulation of
commodities via the exchange process which distributes output –
means of production, raw materials and consumer goods – to users in

213

such a way that the production process can re-commence on an expanded scale.

There has been considerable debate in socialist countries about the extent to which a socialist economy is characterised by generalised commodity production in the sense that all goods produced possess a definite exchange value *vis à vis* all other goods.[1] Nevertheless, because of the essential unity of the processes of production and circulation, it is just as important to focus on the development of exchange (the growth of a national and international market) in explaining growth, as on the production of an economic surplus, since it is only through the extension of the market that the division of labour can develop.

The 'plan versus market' debate is about the mechanism by which the structure of investment and intersectoral balances of a socialist economy are determined. In a capitalist economy, this mechanism is the profit motive. In the writings of Adam Smith this was based on his particular assumptions about human nature (the propensity to 'truck and barter', the self-interestedness of economic activity). For Marx, the mechanism was the same, but driven by the less subjective factor of capitalist competition, the struggle for survival, instead of human 'propensities'. In socialist systems, competition has traditionally been frowned upon as a bourgeois relic, something which perpetuates inequalities of wealth and private monopoly of the means of production. Whether the nature of competition is fundamentally altered if the means of production are publicly owned is a question which until recently has been seriously addressed only by a minority of thinkers. Yet socialist societies have always had problems of achieving investment effectiveness and in generating technological progress, two aspects of growth which competition has encouraged in the capitalist world. The recent waves of economic reform, in which competition plays an important role, are part of the search to bring new pressures to bear so that extension of the market will be translated into further division of labour.

In Vietnam, as in most socialist countries, economic debate has increasingly focused on this problem of finding the most effective mechanism for resource allocation within a socialist framework. The conservative position was that resource allocation in a centrally-planned economy was carried out via the system of material balancing and by issuing central directives about the physical inputs and outputs of individual enterprises. Commodity production was regarded as a transitional form. The 'law of value' would be replaced in the 'socialist' system by prices which were a subsidiary form of cost accounting with no role in resource allocation, this being purely a function of central management decisions. While the role of commodities and prices remains a contentious issue in socialist countries, there is now fairly general agreement that prices do have a wider role. In the first place, during the transition from capitalism to communism, commodity relations inevitably play a role. In the second place, and this is a more radical departure from the traditional view, it is recognised that prices do influence the responses of workers and managers to plan directives and hence the ability of the economy to reach the planned physical proportions.

Prices form the link, then, between the sphere of production and that of circulation and distribution. It is not only the role of prices in equilibrating supply and demand that is important here, but also their role in distributing profits (or surplus) between industries and sectors and in providing incentives to producers which affect the structure of production and division of labour. Under the more traditional methods of administrative planning, the prices set often provided signals to producers which contradicted the aims of central plan directives. As a consequence, there has been a growing tendency to argue that prices should bear a closer relation to real costs of production (exchange values) and administrative methods have often been replaced by the use of price incentives (including remuneration systems) as a means of *indirect* planning. This has necessarily involved the devolution of investment and pricing decisions to local levels of administration.[2]

The question of the extent to which economic decision-making should be decentralised is still controversial in Vietnam, but there does seem to be widespread agreement that the economic reforms introduced since 1979 have been a successful mechanism for overcoming the crisis of disproportionality which affected the economy during the late 1970s. This does not mean that planning has been abrogated, however, merely that more indirect forms are utilised.

The reforms to the system of economic management and accompanying changes in the strategic objectives embodied in the Five Year Plans since 1982 had the common aim of developing exchange and the division of labour in the Vietnamese economy. The use of product contracts in agriculture, one of the main planks of the reformed system, was specifically aimed at expanding the marketed surplus in that sector. The possibility that accumulation of surpluses by households rather than by the collective and state institutions would follow was a subordinate consideration to the goal of achieving a reduction in autarky and increased *socialisation* of production which, as always, was considered an essential pre-condition for the development of socialism. In fact private accumulation can be partly controlled through taxation and by restricting the ability of individuals to acquire modern means of production as private property, thereby reducing the danger of re-emerging class exploitation.

On the other hand, if the new incentive system was to succeed in increasing marketable output, the industrial sector must be able to meet the demand for goods to exchange. Therefore it was essential to get the investment strategy right. Handicraft and light industrial installations were particularly important here because for a relatively low investment they could rapidly increase the supply of essential consumer goods and improved implements. As for investment in large-scale projects, it would be concentrated in overcoming a number of key bottlenecks like electricity or transport rather than in a large number of new projects aimed at making heavy industry the 'leading link'.

The problem of integrating the Southern part of the country added an important dimension to the problem after 1975 because the degree of interdependence via commodity exchange was already much further advanced in the South than in the North. Provision of generous American commodity aid had created the conditions under which growth of agricultural surpluses could lead to rapid expansion of the market and a more comprehensive division of labour in Southern Vietnam. However, the development of exchange (influencing structure of production in Vietnam) remained mainly on an international level while local manufacturing was unable to expand. Most of the consumer goods, machinery and modern inputs which Mekong delta peasants became accustomed to using were imported. Paradoxically, then it was the more advanced division of labour within South Vietnam which rendered the economy more vulnerable to structural dislocation and political instability in the wake of the American aid withdrawal after 1975.

At the same time, a powerful commercial class had emerged in South Vietnam under the auspices of the commercial aid programme. These people were able to continue operating in the immediate post-war period and made the implementation of administrative planning and pricing too difficult. Because of the acute shortages and low official prices, southern capitalists were able to circumvent Government efforts to control the supply of rice and other essential commodities. Even after a major clampdown on the activities of 'speculators' and 'hoarders' in May 1978, the unorganised market continued to be the main avenue of distribution of goods in the Nam Bo region.

The situation in the two halves of the country in the mid-1970s can be summarised as follows:

(i)   In the North, the predominant area of economic activity, agriculture, was characterised by a somewhat restricted development of the market and of the division of labour. The heavy industry priority of the DRV Government had led to the creation of a rather autarkic industrial sector, lacking linkages with the domestic economy. Industry also suffered from wartime setbacks, management and labour productivity problems and structural dislocation due to the growing problems with China, previously a major supplier of aid and markets. On the other hand, in spite of the low level of productive forces, the balance of ownership had shifted to State and collective forms. One could say that the major problem facing the regime in the North was to find a way forward to deepen the social division of labour to lay the foundations on which social appropriation and distribution of surpluses could be built. This involved changing both the form and the mechanism of social appropriation (more local autonomy, less administrative intervention) in an attempt to eliminate conflicts of interest between households, collective institutions and the State.

(ii) In the South, the combination of NLF-sponsored revolutionary transformation of land tenure and the extension of commodity exchange under the American economic and military umbrella had given rise to a situation where the division of labour, in the sense that production is specialised and primarily for exchange, was developed to a far greater degree than in the North. However, the system of appropriation in the South was mainly private. Here then, the problem was not only one of designing a policy to deepen and extend the division of labour, but how to widen the command over appropriation and distribution of surpluses to include State and collective agencies rather than just individuals.

The reforms introduced to the various socialist economic mechanisms and the concomitant adjustments to the development strategy were therefore attempting to tackle two different problems. Not surprisingly, given the enormous regional differences confronting policy makers at the outset, the results have also differed from one part of the country to another. While there it little doubt about the marked improvement in overall economic performance since 1979–80, it is not yet possible to describe the Vietnamese economy as unified in the sense of the division of labour being extended to a nation-wide scale. In concluding the analysis of this book I will examine the regional differentiation in the growth process and the major sources of potential for eventually achieving an integrated national market.

REGIONAL DIFFERENTIATION OF GROWTH

Since unification, Vietnamese writing on growth has tended to concentrate on development of the whole country, or on specific problems of regions (such as the problems of grain procurement in An Giang or manioc processing in Tay Ninh). The issue of the economic performance of the North as a whole, by comparison with the South as a whole, is relatively unexplored in official publications and therefore it has been rather difficult to obtain direct comparative data, especially where industry is concerned. Only recently has official recognition that local autarky, by restricting industry-agriculture exchanges, is a problem, particularly in the rural areas of the North, led to a clear focus on the relationship between commodity exchange and the division of labour. On both counts then, the kind of data which can be used to support the arguments being developed here are not readily available and tend to be fragmentary. However, it is possible to obtain some information in support of the argument that prior to 1975, the social division of labour between industry and agriculture was less developed in North Vietnam than in the South and that this unevenness in the pattern of growth has yet to be overcome. The consequence of the restricted specialisation achieved has been that the severe disproportions characterising the earlier phase of development in the DRV have not been removed. While greater balance has emerged in the economy of the Southern region, it has not been possible to achieve on a national scale the balance envisaged in the Party's espousal of the 'economic complementarity' thesis.

The first indicator of the regional variation to be considered is the level of foodgrain marketing. Some idea of the trend in Northern Vietnam can be obtained from figures on foodgrain production and state procurement set out in Table 7.1. I have used foodgrain here as an indication of the overall level of marketing because it includes the crops which constitute the main rural activity in nearly all areas and because it is the only indicator for which comparative data between North and South are available. However, it should be noted that where cash crops and livestock (including those produced in the family economy) are significant elements, the overall level of marketing will be higher. Until now this is more likely to be the case in richer cooperatives where per capita grain production levels are more than sufficient to assure peasant

Table 7.1 Staple grain production and State procurement in
the DRV (paddy equivalent)

	Production 000 t	Procurement 000 t	Procurement share %
1955*	3523.4	681.7	19.3
1957*	3948.0	590.4	14.9
1959*	5192.6	852.7	16.4
1960	4212.0	782.0	18.7
1965	5562.0	1124.9	20.2
1974	6276.6	1013.6	16.1
1975	5490.6	787.2	14.3

*Paddy only.
Source   Vo Nhan Tri, *Croissance Économique de la
Republique Démocratique du Vietnam* (Hanoi: FLPH, 1967)
pp. 215, 245, 293, 337, 426, 451; General Statistical Office,
*Tinh Hinh Phat Trien Kinh Te Va Van Hoa Mien Bac Xa Hoi
Chu Nghia Viet Nam 1960–1975*, Hanoi, 1978, pp. 120, 132.

subsistence, and surplus grain can be used as livestock fodder. In other
words, where grain marketing is higher the marketing of other agricultural products is also likely to be higher. Grain marketing will become a
less useful indicator as regional crop specialisation increases.

One shortcoming of the data in the table is that the figures on
procurement include grain procured as agricultural tax – at that time
officially set at around 15 per cent of the crop. Planned taxes were
rarely collected however: Christine White puts the actual tax rate in
1962 at 7.2 per cent of total food output.[3] Assuming that this did not
increase, an estimate of the share of grain output actually sold to the
State would therefore fall in the range 7.5 per cent to 13 per cent. Prior
to 1960, these figures are not a very good indication of the total
marketed grain because the State, at that time, did not control the
entire wholesale trade, and even after collectivisation its share of the
retail trade grew only slowly.[4] Rice and salt, though, were in a special
category: from 1955 the number of retailers specialising in these two
commodities was limited and their transformation into retailers of the
State trade was set in motion.[5] State monopoly of the grain trade was
therefore established quite early.

For a more comprehensive view of agricultural marketing, including
livestock and cash crop production, it is necessary to use figures in
value terms.[6] Some limited data have been published for the early 1960s
in the North: they show that the value of agricultural produce sold to
the State averaged 16.7 per cent in 1960–5, fell to 15.6 per cent during

the years of escalation around 1966–70 and rose to nearly 22 per cent in 1970–5.[7] Interestingly, the first two periods were those in which private (or unorganised) trade was also very low: according to official data it covered less than ten per cent of retail and wholesale trade, rising after 1970 to nearly 20 per cent[8] – confirming the complementarity of household and collective economies. This means that between 1960 and 1970 somewhat less than 20 per cent of total agricultural output was (legally) marketed while from 1970–5 the proportion rose to just over a quarter. By this time, however, the combined effects of shortages of industrial goods and low procurement prices had led to the revival of parallel markets. While there is no data on the extent to which this affected the grain trade, we must presume that the actual share of marketed grain was slightly higher than the official figures suggest.

For the period after 1975 no separate figures on procurement or marketing in the North are published. Table 7.2 gives data culled from various sources on grain-marketing for a number of North Vietnamese cooperatives. These data are for cooperatives which were regarded as 'models' in the 1970s – indeed three of them (Dinh Cong, Vu Thang and Thang Long) are counted among the most famous 'model' or 'advanced' cooperatives and we must therefore regard their perform-ance as far above the average – even compared with other progressive cooperatives in the North. As mentioned in Chapter 5, the category of 'advanced' represented only about five per cent of Northern coopera-tives. Unfortunately I have not been able to find equivalent data for the post-reform period, but these figures can still usefully be compared with data from the South.

In only three of these examples from the North can it be said that the marketed grain surplus approached Ngo Vinh Long's estimate of the *average* share (50 per cent) in the Mekong delta region in 1970 (although in one the inclusion of non-grain foodstuffs clouds the picture).[9] However, the proportion of grain marketed in the Mekong delta had dropped by the late 1970s to about one-third.[10] The cause of this decline, as we have seen in earlier chapters, was the drying up of the supply of consumer goods and inputs in the wake of American aid withdrawal, leading peasants to reduce output levels and to a more than proportionate drop in marketed surpluses. Efforts by the southern authorities to replace the prevailing market system by planned resource allocation were, in a situation of acute shortages, increasingly sub-verted by black marketeering and speculation by both wealthier traders and corrupt cadres. Low official purchasing prices of grain discouraged individual farmers from selling grain to the State (a) because they could obtain higher prices from private traders and (b) because the State did

Table 7.2 Foodgrain marketing in advanced cooperatives of Northern Vietnam in the 1970s

	Date	State purchases as share of paddy output %
1. My Tho cooperative* (Ha Nam Ninh)	1975	31
	1976	33
	1977†	45
2. Dinh Cong cooperative (Thanh Hoa)	1970	24.1
	1976	35.0
3. Hai Van cooperative (Ha Nam Ninh)	1973	2.3
	1978	15.2
		Commodity grain as share of output value
4. Thang Long cooperative (Hai Hung)	1978†	51.5
		Commodity food value as share of income from agriculture§
5. Quang Nap cooperative (province not specified)	1973	26.1
	1976	33.9
6. Vu Thang cooperative (Thai Binh)	1974	62.9
	1977	71.7

*Figures for My Tho are estimates based on total procurement less 7% tax; †Winter-spring crop only; §Includes livestock production and sales.
Sources Vietnamese Studies, no. 51, pp. 195–6; Vien Su Hoc, *Nong Dan Viet Nam Tien Len Chu Nghia Xa Hoi*, Hanoi: *Nha Xuat Ban Khoa Hoc Xa Hoi*, 1979, pp. 134, 138, 365, 372–3, 378–9; Francois Houtart and Geneviève Lemercinier, *Sociologie d'une Commune Vietnamienne*, CRSR, Louvain-la-Neuve: Université Catholique de Louvain, 1981, p. 47.

not control a sufficient quantity of necessary consumer goods and farm inputs to satisfy farmers' demands.

Where farmers resorted to the free market the effect was to undermine both the Government's equity goals, since the market allocates resources according to wealth, and its planning and accumulation objectives, since it effectively lost control over the marketed grain surplus, leaving it in the hands of local capitalists. The latter had already displayed an ability in commercial activity, hoarding of gold and speculative activities and were in any case discouraged by Government policy of the late seventies from undertaking more productive enterprise. Speculation by private merchants boosted inflationary pressure and worsened the cost of living for urban workers on fixed salaries. The overall effect was a lack of incentive for farmers to increase output.

While the recovery in output and State procurement has been evident in both regions since the reform process began, there are many indications that this has taken place largely in the South.

According to official output and population statistics, average per capita foodgrain production in 1984 was 304 kg of paddy equivalent (compared to little more than 200 kg in 1976). This leaves a fairly comfortable margin above the 240 kg normally given as the subsistence minimum. But Vietnamese officials are not complacent: if allowance is made for seed requirements, storage losses and reserves, the figure of 300 kg per capita can barely be described as a minimum output requirement and there is little safety margin, given the still high population growth-rate. By 1987, the per capita output had fallen again to 280 kg after a series of bad seasons, especially in the North. The Government would like to increase this figure to 400 kg by 1990 so that more grain can be used for livestock feed (especially secondary grain crops like maize) and for export, as well as providing better security of food stocks, but this would mean a 50 per cent output increase in three years and seems very unlikely.

The continuing emphasis in the Five Year Plan for 1986–90 on food production has an additional rationale, namely, the very uneven development of food production throughout the country. In addition to the three main cities (Hanoi, Haiphong and Ho Chi Minh City) and the Special Economic Zone of Vung Tau-Con Dao, no less than 19 of Vietnam's 36 provinces were still, in 1984, producing less than 300 kg per capita. A further eight could be described as barely self-sufficient. In the nine provinces of the Mekong delta region, on the other hand, average per capita output of foodgrain in 1984 was 511 kg and the area produced a surplus to its own consumption needs (measured at 300 kg per capita) of over 3 million tonnes (Table 7.3).

If the living standards of the vast majority of Vietnamese are to reach a reasonable level a number of alternatives are available: (i) further efforts must be made to increase food production in the deficit areas, (ii) the surplus rice produced in the far south of the country must be able to reach the North, or (iii) increased export income must be used to import food supplies. At the present time there are a number of obstacles in the way of the second objective. One is that surpluses in the

Table 7.3 Distribution of food surplus and deficit by region (000 tonnes)

	1976	1982	1984
Hanoi-Haiphong	−236.2	−515.0	−643.2
Northern midlands and highlands	−800.4	−573.2	−603.1
Red River delta	257.9	368.6	57.3
Central coast	−1 070.0	−739.4	−632.6
Central highlands	−47.7	−61.4	−2.9
Eastern Nam Bo	−148.8	−152.8	−96.7
Ho Chi Minh City−Vung Tau	−904.6	−858.6	−848.6
Mekong delta	1 671.9	2 129.1	3 001.2
Net surplus/deficit	−1 228.0	−403.8	231.3
Former DRV*	−1 343.5	−1 211.0	−1 640.6
Former RVN	−308.4	808.4	1 871.9

*Includes Binh Tri Thien province which contains former RVN provinces of Quang Tri and Thua Thien.
Sources So Lieu Thong Ke, 1982, pp. 11–12, 56–7; *1930–84*, pp. 13–14, 90–1.

South are still considered barely sufficient for the region's own needs, especially those of Ho Chi Minh City: another is the shortage of coastal shipping (see p. 234).

If subsidisation of deficit areas from the State budget is to be avoided, the income levels of these areas will need to be raised through development of cash crops or manufacturing industry for export. Recent moves to increase local financial autonomy and encourage regional and handicraft industries have been accompanied by stress on self-provisioning in food by districts and provinces. A decree of mid-1982 announced that in future, only the needs of the regular armed forces would be looked after by the central Government trade network.[11] In the short-term this policy may cause some difficulties, especially in some of the eight provinces which have not yet reached a per capita output of 240 kg.[12] Northern farmers have complained that they cannot move into potentially more lucrative crops because poor transport and storage facilities are likely to ruin the value of output before it reaches markets.[13] Thus there is a strong impetus to continued self-sufficiency in production, in spite of unfavourable conditions. The only southern province in this group, however, is Song Be which, because of its proximity to the Mekong delta and to markets for cash crops in Ho Chi Minh City, has actually reduced its paddy area by 15 per cent since 1980. Ho Chi Minh City itself has adopted a plan to cut its paddy area in half by 1990 and to concentrate agricultural efforts on growing vegetables, industrial and export crops.

Table 7.3 summarises clearly the nature of the food problem in Vietnam. While it shows some improvement in per capita production in most areas in the 1980s, only two areas have consistently produced a surplus over and above the critical 300 kg per capita mark: the Red River delta and the Mekong delta. Yet it is only by going above this subsistence mark that rapid increases in marketed grain can reasonably be expected. In the case of the Red River delta, the surplus is precarious, as is shown by the figures for 1984, when in a rather poor season it was almost wiped out.

In the northern highland and midland provinces, home of nearly 11 million people in 1984, there is no noticeable decline in the grain deficit since 1982, in spite of increased output levels under the product contract system. In the central coastal provinces (which, apart from the cities, constitute the other main deficit area), the rather more rapid improvement is largely accounted for by one province: Quang Nam Da Nang, where a quarter-million tonne deficit in 1976 was turned into a small surplus in 1982 and 1984.

What is implied by the data in Table 7.3 is that per capita output in the former DRV has not risen since 1976 (averaging only 246 kg in 1984) while in the former RVN it has risen rapidly. Even more importantly from the point of view of marketed grain surpluses, *rural* per capita output has risen, according to official statistics, by only 0.35 per cent per annum in the northern half of the country, compared with just over one per cent per annum for the whole country.[14] This situation is most starkly illustrated in the case of the Red River delta rice bowl, where, although land yields have risen since 1976, output per capita has tended to stagnate or even decline (see Table 7.4 for comparative growth rates of population and foodgrain output).

One thing that Table 7.4 brings out, however, is that Northern grain production has developed very unevenly. Growth rates in the period 1980–84 (after the reforms were introduced) are well above those for the whole period from 1976–84, also suggesting strong per capita growth of output at this time. After 1982, however, output slumped. The reason for this may simply be a string of poor seasons – a two-year time period is not long enough to draw any conclusions about the trend rate of growth and we have no separate data for the North in subsequent years. But given that output for the whole country has stagnated around the 17.5–18.5 million tonne mark in 1985–7,[15] it may

Table 7.4 Growth rates of population, foodgrain output and livestock
production by region (% per annum)

Region	Population		Foodgrain output		Pig population
	1976–84	1976–84	1980–84	1982–84	1980–84
Hanoi-Haiphong	5.7	1.0	4.6	1.4	4.6
Northern midlands and highlands	1.1	2.5	4.4	2.4	4.3
Red River delta	1.6	0.3	4.9	−4.9	1.9
Central coast	2.3	4.7	5.4	3.7	3.9
Central highlands	4.8	6.6	7.4	11.6	13.6
Eastern Nam Bo	2.1	3.4	1.4	6.6	9.7
Ho Chi Minh City– Vung Tau–Con Dao	0.2	4.4	6.9†	5.4	6.2
Mekong delta	3.1	4.8	6.5	9.0	8.8
Former DRV*	2.0	1.9	5.7	−0.5	3.4
Former RVN	2.5	4.9	5.5	8.1	5.5
Total	2.3	3.6	5.6	3.8	4.1

*Includes Binh Tri Thien province which includes part of former RVN.
†Ho Chi Minh City only.
Sources So Lieu Thong Ke, 1979, pp. 56–7; 1982, pp. 56–7; 1930–84, pp.
13–14, 90–1.

turn out that the initial impetus to growth given by the reforms in the
North has already run out of steam.

The picture of southern agriculture given in the table is quite
different. In all areas of the South, with the exception of Ho Chi Minh
City, the population growth rate is over two per cent per annum and
there is even some suggestion that the rate is accelerating: official
estimates of population for 1982 and 1984 give a growth rate for the
Southern provinces of 2.9 per cent (compared with 2.5 per cent for the
whole period 1976–84).[16] At the same time, rates of growth of staple
food output have consistently outstripped the rate of population
growth and also appear to be accelerating.

Livestock production has grown consistently faster in the South as
well, at least since 1980. Growth in livestock production depends
heavily on increasing grain output (unless imported feed is available)
and also has an impact on grain production via provision of organic
fertiliser so the close parallel in the growth-rates is to be expected. In
keeping with this, we would expect to see a tapering of growth in

Northern livestock production during the 1983–4, though I have not been able to find much evidence on this.[17]

Livestock production grew even faster in the South between 1976 and 1980 (11 per cent per annum) because large numbers of breeding pigs (and other animals) were shipped from North to South.[18] This enabled rapid recovery of livestock populations which, as shown in Chapter 3, had been decimated by the war.[19] Nevertheless, it is interesting that this growth was almost exclusively in the central coastal and highland provinces. The average annual growth-rate of the pig population in the Mekong delta during this earlier period was only 1.6 per cent and in fact between 1976 and 1979 the numbers had fallen in five of the nine provinces. Lam Thanh Liem reports widespread slaughtering of livestock during 1978 as a result of falling grain production and the high price of feedgrains which made livestock production unprofitable. The free market was flooded with meat, so much so that a duck could be bought for less than the price of a kilo of rice in provincial markets. Some draught animals were also slaughtered to avoid collectivisation.[20] Since the grain crisis was itself partly a result of collectivisation in the Mekong delta, the rapid growth rates of livestock production recorded after 1980 may be attributed to the results of reform in the economic system.

Livestock numbers can also be a useful indicator of the degree of development of commodity exchange. Pork meat is a major subsistence product for Vietnamese peasants, but pigs are also an important source of cash income. Most pigs are raised under contract by households rather than collectives, the latter usually retaining only breeding stock in order to ensure the maintenance of high yielding varieties. The State attempts to keep a monopoly of the pork market, though unfortunately there are few figures available to indicate the degree to which it has been successful in this aim. One report indicated that state procurement had risen from 23 to 51 per cent of marketed pork meat between 1980 and 1983 in Long An province.[21] Other reports indicate a much improved co-ordination of peasant economic interests with those of the State following the introduction of product contracts.[22] However, a conference on economic management in Ho Chi Minh City in August 1984 recorded that the State still controlled only 35 per cent of the city's retail trade in staples (foodgrain and pork meat).[23]

The indications are, then, that as a result of the reforms both output and marketed surpluses of the main agricultural products have improved greatly, especially in the South. State procurement of those products which it attempts to control has also improved, though also mainly in the South. Compared with the 1960s, there has been some loosening of state control and a concomitant development of free (including black) markets in the North. This is largely due to the continuing food shortages experienced in the northern and central areas and the failure to make adjustments in the official price structure over a long period.[24]

What needs to be explained is why in the South the reform process seems to have unleashed a cumulative expansion of output, while in the North the initial spurt of growth after the poor harvests of 1977–80 appears to have petered out after 1982.

The first possible explanation is the weather. Both the northern and central delta plains are subject to severe weather conditions and this cannot be discounted as a major cause of crop setbacks. In most years since 1983 there have been serious crop losses because of cold spells, drought and typhoons. Indeed this is precisely the reason why, in Vietnamese thinking on economic reunification, so much stress has been laid on developing southern agricultural potential: the Mekong delta has a milder climate and more fertile soil. However, the vulnerability of North Vietnamese crops to the vagaries of the weather could be ameliorated by improvements in the technical level of the agricultural sector; for example, through better water control, development of drought- and cold-resistant varieties, pest- and disease-resistant varieties, etc. Some progress has already been made in this direction, but widespread adoption of many of the new techniques will have to await a much higher level of mechanisation and availability of modern inputs.

This brings me to the second explanation of the relatively poor performance of Northern agriculture which lies in the more backward development of the social division of labour compared with the southern part of the country. In Chapter 5 I argued that although the Vietamese leadership paid lip-service to Lenin's warning that large-scale collective farming could not be achieved without industrialisation, the dominant group among these leaders tended to ignore it in practice. Where more orthodox Marxists have argued that socialisation of production via a qualitative increase in the division of labour is a necessary pre-condition for consolidating socialism, Vietnamese leaders were often closer to the Maoist conception that changes in ownership relations could themselves force an advance in technology and organisation of production.[25]

While increases in output were undoubtedly achieved via reorganisation of the labour force in the collectives, the new technical division of labour was not similar to that of modern industry and did not lead to economies of scale in the longer term. Moreover, as was shown in Chapter 6, the industrial development strategy adopted by the DRV tended to neglect the importance of the division of labour in the sense of developing national and international commodity exchange. Instead, both pricing policies and investment strategies favoured conditions for semi-autarkic expanded reproduction within in the heavy industry sector at the expense of growth in agriculture and light industry. No serious remedy for this situation was begun until the 1979 reforms.

Southern agriculture, by contrast, had benefited in the last years of the Thieu regime from a massive injection of modern inputs and consumer goods which enabled it to achieve rapid expansion of output. The small industrial sector of the South was also geared towards the domestic consumer market – though admittedly more towards the urban middle-class market than towards meeting the needs of peasants. Both sectors suffered structural dislocation following the withdrawal of American aid. The acute foreign exchange shortage after April 1975 warranted policies to reduce the level of imports and increase exports, and in order to restore growth many previously imported consumer goods and raw materials would need to be replaced by domestically produced goods. The new Government made strenuous efforts from the outset to reorganise industrial production, to reduce the imported component of raw materials and to meet the input and consumption needs of the peasantry and to increase exports. In addition, substantial quantities of goods were moved from North to South in order to minimise the dislocation to the two sectors.

The South Vietnamese engineering industry, for example, had previously concentrated on assembly of imported components, but by 1976 it was producing 12-horsepower tractors (the same model produced in the North's Tran Hung Dao Engineering Works), the Sinco [Singer] Sewing Machine Company was making spare parts for mechanical saws, Vicasa (iron-rolling mills) were recycling scrap iron from discarded US war materiel, the South Vietnam Discarded Materials Company was using the same type of materials to produce farm tools and spare parts, as well as repairing vehicles, pumps and generators. A number of small fertiliser plants were producing lime (from Ha Tien) or grinding Lao Cai (North Vietnam) apatite ore for phosphate fertiliser. The sugar and food processing industries, which had previously relied heavily on imported inputs, had switched a substantial share of production to domestic raw materials. Cogido paper mill at Bien Hoa, which had previously imported most of its raw material had shifted to 75 per cent locally-produced materials by mid-1976. And there was also a substantial shift from using goods made from imported materials like plastic, to more traditional handicraft goods like rattan, palm leaf, reed and wooden articles.[26] Ex-prostitutes and ex-drug addicts, middle-class wives of Thieu-regime officials and the unemployed were organised into handicraft cooperatives, producing goods from local and imported raw materials for export.

While the shortages of manufactured goods were not eliminated in this way, the South did have a headstart in restoring the previously high levels of urban-rural commodity exchange (and moreover reducing import-dependency). The process was facilitated by the fact that the South did not have large amounts of resources tied up in the construction of heavy industry projects, but at the same time it was hindered, especially during 1977–8, by the application of inappropriate pricing and incentive systems.

Some more examples illustrate the way in which the southern industrial structure has been closely linked to agricultural development. Outside the Saigon-Bien Hoa area in the 1970s there was very little industrial activity at all. In 1972, for example, An Xuyen province (now part of Minh Hai) had thirty-two rice mills, three print shops, two ice plants and two ice cream machines, two sawmills and two workshops repairing machinery, boats and cars. By 1983 there was far greater diversification: Minh Hai had 63 state enterprises (46 central, 17 at provincial level and below) and about 500 handicraft groups producing electricity, hand-tools, medicines, soap, bricks, timber, boats, salt, seafood, fish sauce, textiles, and books.[27] Other Mekong delta provinces are producing agricultural machinery, wheel-frames, tyre-tubes, ploughs and harrows, pumps, hand-tools, spare parts, pumps, medicines, rice flour, printer's ink, soap, bricks, tiles, sawn timber, white spirit, ice, sugar, frozen and dried seafood, fish sauce, salt, canned fruit, soybean paste and tofu, Vietnamese speciality foods, mosquito netting, silk cloth, towels, coir ropes and matting, carpets, garments, books, lacquer ware, bamboo and rattan ware, wooden articles, electricity, river sand, stone and many more.[28] There is a multitude of machine repair shops. Outside Ho Chi Minh City and the Vung Tau-Con Dao Special Zone, only Dong Nai province, containing the industrial centre of Bien Hoa, and Ha Tien with its cement works have any significant development of modern industry. The industrial structure is predominantly 'light' and based on utilisation of local raw materials, production of consumer goods or simple agricultural machinery, transport means and goods for export.

While it remains small, the industry of the Mekong delta provinces is, therefore, strongly tied to the production of basic consumer goods, exports and inputs for agriculture. But Ho Chi Minh City is by far the most important industrial centre of the southern region, producing about 30 per cent of total national output. Employment in industry in the city by 1980 was 235 600, only about 14 per cent above the 1974 figure, but the sector has grown rapidly since then: by 1984 industrial employment (including handicraft workers) had risen to 400 000.[29]

The structure of industrial employment is shown in Table 7.5: it can be seen here that the largest employers in 1980 were the machinery (20 per cent of output value in 1984[30]), textile and food processing

Table 7.5 Structure of industrial employment in Ho Chi Minh City in 1980

| | Total | State and joint state-private | | | Co-op | Production group | Individual and private |
		Centre	City	District			
No. of enterprises	24 732	189	188	50	202	1951	22 192
Average workers per enterprise	9.5	269	215	29	135	24	3
% of workers in:							
Energy	0.5	0.4	0.1	0.0	0.0	0.0	0.0
Metallurgy	0.6	0.6	0.0	0.0	0.0	0.0	0.0
Machinery	18.7	0.6	3.8	0.2	1.1	3.5	9.4
Chemicals	12.6	4.4	2.6	–	0.2	2.2	3.2
Construction materials, ceramics and glass	10.4	1.5	1.7	0.3	1.2	2.7	3.0
Food processing	15.4	4.5	1.7	0.1	–	2.3	6.9
Textiles	32.0	9.1	5.0	–	7.4	7.3	3.2
Cultural products	7.2	0.3	1.5	–	1.7	1.8	2.0
Miscellaneous	2.4	0.0	0.8	0.0	0.0	0.5	1.1
Total	100.0	21.5	17.2	0.6	11.6	20.2	28.8

Note – represents 0.05% or less. Columns do not always add due to rounding errors.
Source Ho Duc Hung, *Cong Nghiep Phuc Vu Nong Nghiep* (Industry Serving Agriculture), Ho Chi Minh City: *Nha Xuat Ban Thanh Pho Ho Chi Minh*, 1984, pp 33–4.

branches, followed by chemicals, construction materials, ceramics and glass. Apart from the Ha Tien cement works (in Kien Giang province), the Vicasa iron works in Ho Chi Minh City was the only important heavy industry installation in the South. There is little indication that this structure has changed very much since 1980 except for a slight increase, by 1984, in favour of cooperatives.[31] The cooperative sector employed 16 per cent of the city's industrial workforce and produced 23 per cent of its output in 1984. Since then, more encouragement has also been given to small, privately-owned firms employing wage labour, the scale and scope of such activities to be determined according to the type of product.[32]

The structure of industry in the city is thus rather similar to that of the Mekong delta provinces, in the sense that it is geared to the needs of the rural and export sectors and consumer demand. The role of the Ho Chi Minh City industrial sector in the development of the national economy is perceived in a rather different light to that of the North. Whereas official references to Northern industry have stressed the heavy industry and energy base, Ho Chi Minh City officials have dwelt on the importance of supplying light industrial goods to peasants as part of developing the division of labour between agriculture and industry, both to modernise agriculture and to increase the supply of consumer goods and export income for the expansion of industry itself. One publication set out the role of industry in the city as follows:[33]

(1) ... to realise the scientific and technical revolution in agriculture through electrification, mechanisation and chemicalisation ... and to contribute to speeding up the process of socialist transformation and social division of labour in agriculture;

(2) ... to contribute to the development of production of agricultural commodities by supplying means of production (hand tools, capital equipment, fertiliser, insecticide) to agriculture;

(3) ... to process agricultural products in order to guarantee their effective use and to increase the value of agricultural commodities to serve consumption and exports;

(4) ... to produce consumer goods to raise the material and spiritual welfare of the peasants and positively develop the exchange of goods between industry of the city and agriculture of the outlying districts;

(5) ... to create the conditions for agriculture to move gradually towards the production and management model of industry.

The increase in the exchange of commodities between the industries of

Ho Chi Minh City and the rural sectors of the Mekong delta and Eastern Nam Bo has, in my view, been the major cause of the acceleration of growth in the southern region, at a time when the effect of the economic reforms appears to be diminishing in the northern half of the country. This essential pre-condition for a resumption of growth has been provided by the reforms, but a key element in the renewed dynamism of the South Vietnamese economy has been the emphasis in the development strategy on the division of labour between industry and agriculture. The *source* of economic growth has been the utilisation of marketed agricultural surplus to increase exports and expand the industrial base while using industrial output and export income to modernise agriculture and provide incentives (both individual and collective) to the peasants, so that they in turn expand output and marketed surpluses further. While the administrative planning system transferred from the North during the first four years after 1975 failed to achieve the goals of that development strategy, the economic reforms, through a better mixture of price incentives and encouraging greater local initiative in adjusting the output mix to meet changes in demand, have provided the mechanism that was needed.

In the North, however, the industrial structure, in spite of some changes since 1982, remains concentrated in heavy industry. While this is not in itself detrimental to agricultural development in the long run, the longer gestation periods and teething problems experienced by many of these projects have meant that, even after the adjustments made to investment and output mix, the increase in the supply of commodities to the rural sector has been slow to eventuate. For example, the Da River hydro-electric scheme, into which much of the 30 per cent of industrial investment devoted to power generation in the 1981-5 plan was sunk, is not due for completion until 1990. Expansion of Lam Thao fertiliser plant, designed to double the existing output of superphosphate, was not completed until 1984. Bim Son cement factory, phase one of which – with a design capacity of 600 000 tonnes per annum – was completed in early 1982, but managed to produce only 800 000 tonnes in nearly three years of operation.[34]

The shortages of such basic industrial goods as fuel and fertiliser hampers the growth of marketed surpluses in northern agriculture. A remedy could be provided by imports following increased export earnings from the rural and handicraft sectors, but a key factor inhibiting the rapid growth of commodity exchange between agriculture and industry has been the fact that despite growth of output in 1980–4, per capita production levels in the North have not yet reached a point where minimum consumption requirements of the rural population can safely be guaranteed. The combination of continuing 'goods famine' and low marketed agricultural surplus in the North has thus lessened the impact of the economic reform on the overall rate of growth.

OUTLOOK FOR AN INTEGRATED NATIONAL MARKET

Over a decade after the end of the Vietnam War, it appears that the two halves of the country have remained substantially separate in terms of their economic development. In the South, particularly the far south around the Mekong delta and Ho Chi Minh City, the close linkage of agriculture and light industrial development has given the impetus to sustain economic growth in the 1980s. But the North is still apparently plagued by the legacy of war damage and over-concentration of industrial investment in heavy industry projects which have held back the rise of living standards and the deepening of the social division of labour.

However, the picture is not as simple as that. In the past decade, the greater dynamism of the Southern economy has been underpinned, to a considerable extent, by 'aid' from the North. The restoration and restructuring of production in the South following the US withdrawal was in part made possible by the transfer of large quantities of goods of Northern origin. In fact the 'aid' took the form of very one-sided trade between the two regions.

In the first twelve months after April 1975, the North exported 1.6 million tonnes of goods and raw materials to the South – including rice, sugar, fuel, pesticides, fertiliser (including apatite ore), chemicals, medicine, cloth, seeds, livestock, buses, chinaware, farm tools, fishing boats, building materials, motors and generators, tractors, bulldozers, water pumps, spare parts – and large numbers of technical cadres and skilled workers.[35] Doubtless some of the goods actually originated abroad (particularly fuel), but much was also produced in North Vietnam itself and, as such, this trade with the South did nothing to alleviate the shortages being experienced in the North. South Vietnamese exports to the North in this period amounted to only 80 000 tonnes. To these figures we should add an unknown, but probably not very large, volume of unrecorded trade by Vietnamese travelling across the former divide to visit relatives and friends after years of forced separation.

In the longer run, greater balance in the Northern economy may itself depend on the development of exchange between the North and South. If the expansion of Southern agricultural and light industrial capacity which has been set in motion by the reforms continues, then the role envisaged for it in the Party's 'economic complementarity thesis' may indeed come to fruition. Similarly, the development of heavy industry in the North, provided it is based on a realistic assessment of the resources available in the country and those which it would be better to purchase abroad (at least for the time being), could become the basis for growth of agriculture and consumer industries in the South.

Since political unification in 1976 information on North-South trade has not been readily available. My requests to meet Home Trade Ministry officials were not fulfilled and I have not been able to find published sources, so this gap cannot yet be filled. In general, however, the level of trade remains weak. This is partly owing to the poor development of transport infrastructure (though this remains one of the chief investment priorities).[36] However, another important reason is that southern agricultural surpluses are not yet considered high enough to meet the requirements of the South. Per capita output of foodgrains in the former RVN was still only 366 kg in 1984 and though this is above the subsistence minimum, there are many other uses to which rice can be put: a small amount of high quality southern rice is exported to obtain much-needed imported goods and part of the rest is used for alcohol, flour and noodle production or even fed to livestock. In spite of the South's apparent surplus of grain, therefore, the authorities have avoided large-scale shipments to the North in case there are shortages and price increases in the South. When the government did ship 240 000 tonnes to Hanoi in 1987, following a massive 700 000 tonnes shortfall of the Northern spring rice crop, there were indeed reports of dissatisfaction in Ho Chi Minh City.[37]

To the extent that the trade does develop, however, it seems likely that the pattern will involve the shipment south of producer goods (particularly chemical fertiliser, coal, and machinery) in exchange for southern agricultural and light industrial goods. At present the South is still heavily dependent upon imported basic goods (such as fuel, nitrogenous fertiliser) so improved domestic availability should release foreign exchange for growth in other areas. To the extent that these goods are already supplied by Northern industry (phosphate fertiliser or machinery, for example) the 'economic complementarity' of the two regions continues to be a factor in Southern economic growth. By the same token, increased 'exports' of agricultural and consumer goods from South to North would help alleviate the shortages and promote rural growth – especially by encouraging a movement towards specialisation on cash crops and rural industrialisation in those areas less suited to rice production. In the longer run, then, we can expect the division of labour flowing from the extension of commodity exchange between the two regions to play a progressively greater role in economic development.

For the time being, the North remains a 'less developed' region in the sense that in spite of its industrial development, the majority of the population have not experienced rising living standards. Future growth, especially in the medium term will depend upon the southern region acting as a 'growth pole' through its expanding domestic division of labour (involving exchange between industry and agriculture) underpinning a rapid expansion of export income. Given the still small size of the Vietnamese economy, the development of international trading links will be a factor of key importance in further developing the division of labour, increasing labour productivity and accumulation of surpluses.

Foreign trade has, however, been one of the most problematical areas of the Vietnamese economy since 1975. The 'heavy industry priority' strategy with its emphasis on creating a 'self-reliant' industrial structure precluded giving much attention to trade before the 1980s and this pattern of relatively autarkic policy was reinforced in practice by the sharp reduction in external aid after the US defeat and the break with China. Vietnam's capacity to pay for its imports was dramatically reduced, although the expectation that exports would increase under the impact of socialist transformation in the South led to rapidly rising import levels and a debt crisis in the mid-1980s.

This is particularly reflected in the pattern of trade and payments with the non-communist world. Exports to the convertible currency area grew by only two per cent a year from 1976 to 1978 (as against five per cent for all exports), while imports grew at 37 per cent per annum (eight per cent for all imports). Beginning in 1979, the year reforms were introduced in Vietnam, exports to the convertible area picked up, growing at over 12 per cent per annum in 1978–86, while imports stagnated and then fell continuously until 1983.[38] In 1981 Vietnam was reported to have defaulted on loan repayments to the International Monetary Fund.[39] The estimates available show that while the convertible area share of total debt was only about a third in the early 1980s, well over 90 per cent of debt service payments fell into this category between 1978 and 1981.[40] This made it much more urgent to improve the balance of trade with the convertible area, given that restrictions on aid and possibly on rescheduling of debt would continue. The difficulties with the IMF made it unlikely that Vietnam could obtain further loans from multilateral agencies or Western banks.

After the signing of the Treaty of Friendship and Cooperation with the Soviet Union and Vietnam's formal accession to CMEA in June 1978, the opportunity to re-source imports to the industrialised countries of Eastern Europe and to reduce the proportion of high-cost Western debt in the total external debt must have proved attractive to Vietnamese decision-makers. Taking import and export figures together, there has been a marked improvement in Vietnam's trade balance with the hard currency area since 1978 so that the export coverage of imports had risen from 14 per cent to over half by 1985. This improvement has also been strengthened by payments on current account. One aspect of the Vietnamese economic reforms since 1979 has been to encourage overseas Vietnamese to send goods and money, including investment funds, to assist economic recovery. The full extent of this is not quantifiable at present, though one estimate is of an inflow of $US 300 million per annum (about equal to hard currency export earnings).[41] The huge capital outflow represented by the illegal export of gold, which took place at the height of the 'boat people' exodus in 1978–80,[42] has also been largely halted. Officially recorded data on 'services and transfers' show a shift to a small positive balance by 1982–3.[43]

If we can assume that these changes have continued to reinforce the positive changes in trade since 1979, then we can also assume that the growth in convertible currency debt has been slowed and, with it, the extraordinarily high debt service ratio. At the same time the share of Vietnamese trade with CMEA increased after 1978 (though this trend has now been reversed) while imports from CMEA have continued to grow more quickly than exports to CMEA.[44] Whether or not it conforms to Vietnamese plans, this makes good sense because Soviet debt is on better terms than Western debt, given that Vietnam has not had access to 'soft-loan' agencies like the World Bank's IDA. It usually takes the form of 20–30-year loans at 2–3 per cent interest. Borrowing to finance the imports needed for development is therefore more likely to remain a feasible option. The gradual erosion of the Western aid embargo on Vietnam since 1983, however, has enabled Vietnam to obtain some trade credits from countries like South Korea and Japan while there has also been a small amount of foreign investment (for example, in assembly of knocked-down motor cycles and electrical appliances and in construction).[45]

In late 1987 Vietnam passed a new foreign investment law, replacing that of 1977, by which it hopes to attract an increased inflow of capital for export and import-substituting activities. The new law allows up to 100 per cent ownership by the foreign investor (compared with 49 per cent previously), remittance of profits and other income accruing and repatriation of capital upon sale or dissolution (subject to a small tax). The company tax rate is set at 15–25 per cent, with the higher rates reserved for oil, gas and other 'valuable and rare' resources, but tax holidays may be allowed for the first two years, with further reductions possible. Losses may be carried over for tax purposes for up to five years. Partial re-investment of profits entitles the firm to a refund of tax paid on those profits. Enterprises must be 'self-provisioning' in foreign currency: if imported parts or materials are required, sufficient export income must be earned to cover the foreign exchange cost of these. They must also establish a reserve fund of five per cent of profits, and cover social insurance for their workers.[46] Many of the conditions for investment are specifically left open to negotiation with individual firms and, as happened in China, there may turn out to be considerable variations from the law in practice due to the political strength of local officials.

Under the previous foreign investment law, the main investors were CMEA countries – who invested in oil and gas exploration and production, fishing, plantation agriculture (coffee, tea, rubber), joint ventures – and India. There were few Western companies, but greater interest has been shown by potential foreign investors as the Vietnamese economy has begun to grow in the 1980s following the reforms. Vietnam has a cheap and highly-skilled labour force and it is also attractive to some Asian investors as a way to beat Western import quotas on such products as garments. Nevertheless the continuing difficulties of the economy, notably the high rate of inflation, black market in foreign currency, poorly-developed infrastructure and electricity shortages are likely to prevent a flood of investors from arriving. Revived Western interest was already under way before the new law was passed, so it should be seen more as a measure of the anxiety in Vietnam to increase participation in the international division of labour, than as something which will in itself stimulate investment.

The importance of the international division of labour in stimulating productivity growth has now been recognised by the Vietnamese leadership, especially with the elevation of exports to one of the three

238 *National Unification and Economic Development in Vietnam*

major priorities of the 1986–90 plan period and with the strong emphasis on policies to stimulate the production of exportable agricultural crops, handicraft products and manufactured consumer goods. The criteria for investment are that such activities should utilise the abundant natural resources and labour supply of the country and concentrate on areas with relatively low capital requirements in order to achieve maximum effectiveness of the investment. There are also frequent references to the importance of international division of labour and expanding the scope of commodity exchange, with 'cooperation' taking second place in the aims of trade.[47] The Vietnamese continue to stress trade within CMEA (which currently accounts for about two-thirds of the total) and the widespread introduction of reforms within Eastern Europe also raises the possibility of greater specialisation and effectiveness in this trade too.

A start has been made, then, in unravelling some of the contradictions inherent in combining accelerated growth with unification, that is, in overcoming the enormous structural imbalances in the economies of the two regions which were the legacy of two decades of separation and war. The combined effects of a reordering of investment priorities and changing the system of incentives to encourage more competition and local initiative have succeeded in improving the social division of labour and extending the national market.

8 Conclusion

This book has focused on the theme of economic unification in Vietnam since 1975. I have tried to demonstrate that the unification process itself has been a crucial factor determining the course of development.

In so doing, I have taken the discussion of Vietnamese economic development beyond the major themes which have dominated Western scholarship and debate in recent years. Previous approaches to unification and economic development have tended to fall into two camps. On the one hand, discussion of unification has been in terms of military and political changes – the defeat of the Southern regime, the designing of a new constitution and new social and economic policies. Many writers have pointed to the social conflicts engendered by application of the socialist political system in the South or changes in international relations brought about by the new regional balance of power, with a unified Vietnam emerging as a significant military and diplomatic force. Discussion of economic development, on the other hand, has concentrated on the implications of Vietnam's external relations – with the West and, more especially, with the Soviet Union – the legacies of wartime destruction, poor climatic conditions in the north and centre of the country and the inefficiencies of the administrative planning system.

These are all issues which are familiar to students of the socialist world in general. The issues which are not so familiar, however, are those raised by economic unification of regions with incompatible socio-economic systems. These are particularly important questions for the less developed socialist economies, such as North Korea and China, which face the prospect of absorbing very dynamic capitalist economies in the process of reunification. While South Vietnam's economy before 1975 had not taken on the dynamism of South Korea, Hong Kong and Taiwan, we have seen that the foundations for a similar type of development were being laid.

Special interest therefore attaches to Vietnam's experience in undertaking its transition to socialism while attempting to integrate a large capitalist region, comprising approximately half the country, with a socialist region which already has a developed set of socialist institutions and traditions. This added a new and complex set of problems to those already faced by a very underdeveloped economy recently emerged from a protracted war. What I have done in this book, therefore, is to look at the economic foundations of the reunification process, at the ways the two merging economic systems have interacted and affected each other's development.

The Southern economy could not be transformed into a socialist one just by the acquisition of a new system of government and a new set of ownership rules, even though the success of the National Liberation Front's revolution in the South had contributed directly to the defeat of the capitalist regime. The fact that it had been a very open economy, with a highly developed system of commodity exchange, rendered it vulnerable to dislocation upon the withdrawal of the American aid prop. The Northern economy on the other hand, was able to survive wartime destruction and the shock of Chinese aid cuts, partly because of its greater autarky. While the urban population of the North suffered greatly, especially when aid levels were reduced without a concomitant increase in supplies of food coming from the countryside, the degree of dislocation for the much larger urban population of the South was greater because the standard of living, sustained by aid-financed consumer imports had been higher.

In this context the attempt to apply administrative pricing and planning policies in the South was doomed from the outset. Such policies could only be applied successfully in Vietnam under certain conditions. As I argued in Chapters 4 and 5, they were able to produce once-and-for-all increases in output and yields through the mobilisation of labour for labour accumulation projects under conditions of large seasonal labour surpluses and a strong tradition of communal land ownership and cooperative practices in agriculture. Yet they did not operate very effectively as a means of generating continuous increases in agricultural productivity, and in industry they led to an emphasis on over-ambitious investment plans which took little account of the existing input-output relationships as the basis of a balanced economic structure.

In the South the introduction of administrative planning mechanisms also produced a retreat into autarky by the peasantry, except in the central coastal provinces where conditions more nearly corresponded to those of the North two decades earlier and the measures provided an initial boost to output. The failure to raise marketed surpluses in the rich Mekong delta in the late 1970s jeopardised the livelihoods of much of the Southern population – up to sixty per cent of whom depended entirely upon the market for their means of subsistence. It also deprived Vietnam of export income which was urgently needed to overcome the acute dislocation to the circulation of commodities caused by aid withdrawal and set back by several years the potential for solving the food deficit in the North.

The very different socio-economic conditions which had emerged in the South under the colonial regime and over two decades of formal division of the country were, therefore, a crucial element in the severity of the economic crisis which hit Vietnam in the late 1970s.

However, the legacy of separate development in the South has also been advantageous for the resumption of growth and extension of exchange after the introduction of economic reforms. The lack of a heavy industrial sector with its high level of demand for investment funds, the existence of a highly skilled workforce (many of whom obtained their skills in the technologically advanced armed forces of the old Southern regime), the market 'tradition', combined with a rich agricultural potential (in spite of extensive wartime damage to important production zones such as the rubber growing uplands), have all enabled the southern region to use the reforms to maximum effect. The devolution of financial autonomy and establishment of direct trading between enterprises have helped to break down regional barriers to trade and restored the widespread exchange of goods between Ho Chi Minh City and the Mekong delta, as well as enabling regional crop specialisation to take place. This process has been greatly assisted by the existence in the South of a network of waterways (reconstructed after the war) and good roads (built during the war) facilitating the movement of goods. While the reform policies have by no means succeeded in eliminating the problems of shortages/inflation, a good start has been made. If the division of labour in the southern region continues to deepen under the impact of better incentives, productivity can increase further and lead to larger surpluses.

Expansion of demand in the southern regional economy can in turn stimulate the recovery of both the Northern industrial sector, by enabling some branches to take advantages of scale economies previously denied by the small size of the DRV market, and Northern agriculture, by improving the possibilities of exchanging farm products for manufactured consumer goods or rice.

However, a number of other obstacles need to be overcome before an integrated national market can become a tangible reality. One is a dramatic improvement in transport and communications both within the North and between North and South to enhance the viability of abandoning subsistence farming in favour of commodity crops.

Another is the gradual erosion of those bureaucratic 'traditions' and strongholds of regional political autonomy which still enable local administrations to allocate resources according to political criteria – for example, by building prestige projects or restricting development of product specialisation in order to maintain local economic independence. Favouritism and corruption are also sustained by local autarky. The experience of Yugoslavia is a potent reminder of the difficulties which can arise if a restricted set of market reforms are combined with extensive powers of regional political authorities to promote particularism and regional autarky. Inefficient heavy industries ('political factories') are protected, trading links are developed mainly with foreign countries while production for the domestic market suffers from diseconomies and low quality of output due to poor inter-regional integration of the market.

The economic power of local as well as central bureaucracies can be eroded by decentralising many economic decisions to the level of the enterprise or household, by allowing the 'base units' to make their own decisions about investment, product mix, export-import mix and pricing within parameters set by economic policies of the government. This devolution of economic power enables state and collective enterprises to compete effectively with the private sector. But it can also increase the ability of the central government to manage the economy by reducing political interference on the part of lower administrative levels with State objectives, and by delivering rising surpluses to the State plan as the incentive-driven system increases the productivity of land and labour.

The main lesson which emerges from the Vietnamese experience, then, is that the relative autarky and low productivity growth of the 'traditional' socialist economy will not be able to survive the impact of unification with a system of generalised commodity exchange based on competition. Any attempt to impose administrative planning mechanisms on such an economy, even if better prepared than in the Vietnamese case, is likely to destroy the productivity gains that can be had from using an incentive system to build on the existing division of labour. While the effect on South Vietnam was worsened by the dislocation caused by the cut in external resources, the problem of capital flight could cause equally severe problems in the case of a more advanced capitalist economy being absorbed. Unification cannot work if the bureaucracy is too obtrusive. If is sets over-ambitious growth targets and investment rates, shortages and lack of incentives will overwhelm the economy.

Vietnam's experience with unification has also shown that the expansion of commodity exchange, both domestic and international, is a better way to ensure growth and rising economic surpluses than the 'self-reliant' industrialisation models initiated in the socialist world by Stalin and widely adopted by the newly-emerging socialist states in the 1950s and in some Asian states as late as the 1970s.

One problem which Vietnam has never really had to face, is how to deal with a large and powerful capitalist class. The emergence of such a class in South Vietnam had barely begun by the 1970s and, given widespread popular acceptance of the revolutionary forces, the use of monetary and fiscal reforms to weaken the economic power of private capital would have been more successful in stabilising the economy and stimulating economic growth than would administrative measures. The administrative measures used in Vietnam in 1978, as we saw, removed many of the individuals from effective participation in economic life without removing the root causes of speculation and hoarding, the pricing policies of the government. While the existence of major concentrations of economic power in private hands does indeed pose a threat to socialist transformation, it seems unlikely that small capitalists and petty traders or producers could do so. There is therefore considerable scope for allowing these to continue functioning during a prolonged transition period. Provided State-owned and collective sectors are allowed to compete effectively, the hoped-for dominance of the 'socialist' economy can still emerge.

Notes

For abbreviations, refer to list on page xiii–xiv.

Chapter One Introduction

1. See Suzanne Paine, *New Statesman,* November 1985. Politically, the adoption of such an approach in Vietnam was made even less likely by the fact that the acceptance of 'capitalist enclaves' had been suggested by the Chinese at the time of their reconciliation with the United States in 1972. It was taken up by some Americans as a possible way of saving the Thieu regime.

2. Gareth Porter, 'Vietnam's Long Road to Socialism', *Current History,* vol. 71 (1976) p. 211.

3. See Le Duan's Political Report to the 4th Party Congress, held in December 1976, which stated that a principal task of the Second Five Year Plan was to 'achieve basic *socialist transformation* in the South'. Communist Party of Vietnam, *4th National Congress Documents* (Hanoi: FLPH, 1977, p. 63).

4. Possibly the experience of China in the early 1950s in gaining control over the production and trade of Shanghai and the other Treaty Ports was in their minds. The Chinese experience has been described in Xue Muqiao, *China's Socialist Economy* (Beijing: Foreign Languages Press, 1981) pp. 20–30.

5. Communist Party of Vietnam, op. cit., p. 42.

6. Ibid., pp. 27–34, especially pp. 31–34.

7. See Le Chau, *Le Vietnam socialiste: une économie de transition* (Paris: Maspero, 1966) p. 243.

8. For example, the Soviet industrialisation debate of the 1920s, important contributions to which can be found in N. Spulber (ed.), *Foundations of Soviet Strategy for Economic Growth* (Bloomington: University of Indiana Press, 1964) and Richard B. Day (ed.) *Nikolai Bukharin: Selected Writings on the State and the Transition to Socialism* (New York: M. E. Sharpe, 1982). Mao Zedong also discussed this question in his *On Ten Great Relations* Beijing: FLPH.

9. For example, Communist Party of Vietnam, op.cit.: 'the North ... has brilliantly fulfilled its duty as the revolutionary base of the whole country' (p. 26) and 'We have the socialist North, a major material and spiritual force which has accumulated some valuable experience in socialist revolution. In our country as a whole, the forces of socialism are in a position of overwhelming superiority.' (p. 42).

10. For example, Martin J. Murray, *The Development of Capitalism in Colonial Indochina (1870–1940)* (Berkeley: University of California Press, 1980).

11. See, for example, G. Nguyen Tien Hung, *Economic Development of Socialist Vietnam, 1955–80* (New York: Praeger, 1977); Jean Lacouture, *Vietnam: Between the Two Truces* (New York: Vintage, 1966).

Chapter Two   Political Unity and Economic Separation: the Colonial Period

1. G. Nguyen Tien Hung, *Economic Development of Socialist Vietnam 1955–80* (New York: Praeger, 1977) p. 15.
2. See, for example, Charles Robequain, *The Economic Development of French Indochina,* (New York: Oxford University Press, 1944) p. 308.
3. Pierre Gourou, *Les Paysans du Delta Tonkinois* (Paris: Mouton, 1965).
4. Ibid., p. 560 (my translation).
5. Gouvernement Général de l'Indochine, *Rapports au Grand Conseil des Interêts Économiques et Financiers et au Conseil de Gouvernement* (Hanoi: Imprimerie d'Extrême Orient (IDEO), 1930).
6. Robequain, op. cit., p. 247.
7. Le Chau, *Le Vietnam socialiste: une économie de transition* (Paris: Maspero, 1966) pp. 73–74.
8. Robequain, op. cit., p. 252.
9. Ibid., p. 271.
10. Forty-five per cent of total yarn and fabric consumed in Indo-China between the wars was imported directly. One quarter of the remainder (about 14 per cent of the total) was produced by these two factories.
11. Robequain, op. cit., p. 308.
12. Ibid., p. 310.
13. Martin J. Murray, *The Development of Capitalism in Colonial Indochina (1870–1940),* (Berkeley: University of California Press, 1980); Alexander Woodside, *Community and Revolution* (Boston: Houghton Mifflin, 1976); Truong Chinh and Vo Nguyen Giap *The Peasant Question (1937–1938),* Data Paper No. 94 (Ithaca: Cornell University, 1974). Ngo Vinh Long, *Before the Revolution* (Cambridge, Mass.: MIT Press, 1973).
14. In so far as any breakdown of budget receipts could be found for earlier years, the story was similar. For calendar years 1928, 1929 and 1935, the receipts from Registration, Estates and Stamp Duties were:

Year	Cochin China	Annam	Tonkin	Others	Total
	%	%	%	%	%
1928	59.8	2.6	20.0	17.6	100.0
1929	67.5	4.0	21.8	6.7	100.0
1935	56.2	5.3	32.7	5.8	100.0

Source   Rapports au Grand Conseil, 1929, 1930, 1936.

15. Paul Bernard, *Nouveaux Aspects du Problème Economique Indochinois* (Paris: Fernand Sorlot, 1937) p. 52.
16. Paul Bernard, *Le Problème économique indochinois* (Paris: Nouvelles Editions Latines, 1934) p. 14.
17. Archives of the Conseiller aux Affaires économiques, and estimates of population based on Table 2.2.
18. Gouvernement Général de l'Indochine, *Budget Général: Compte Administratif, Exercice 1937* (Hanoi: IDEO, 1938).
19. This was, however, at least an all-weather road the whole way. See

Rapports au Grand Conseil, 1930 (pp. 696–7) and 1938 (pp. 360, 587, 606) for data.

20. Construction of the Chinese section of this line involved a considerable engineering feat, but in the long run, the line, which was run by a private company, was the only profitable one in the whole network.

21. The emphasis here is somewhat different from that of Jean Chesneaux (*The Vietnamese Nation* (Sydney: Current Book Distributors, 1966) p. 116), Murray (op. cit., p. 175) and Virginia Thompson (*French Indo-China* (London: George Allen & Unwin, 1937) p. 206) who stress political and military considerations in railway building.

22. Gouvernement Général, *Budget Général: Compte Administratif 1937,* op. cit.

23. Murray, op. cit., pp. 189, 550.

24. In this case, some indication that only a little redistribution took place is given by the numbers of pupils in secondary education during the 1937–38 school year: Cochin-China 151 439 (31 per cent), Annam 102 237 (21 per cent), Tonkin 167 043 (34 per cent).

25. Robequain, op. cit., p. 152.

26. P. Bernard, *Le Problème économique indochinois,* p. 109.

27. J. R. Andrus, 'Preliminary Survey of the Economy of French Indochina' (U.S. Department of State, June 1945 (mimeo)) p. 112.

28. Gouvernement Général de l'Indochine, *Cochinchine, Compte administratif pour l'Exercice 1930* (Saigon: Imprimerie Nouvelle Albert Portail, 1931).

29. Andrus, op. cit., pp. 110–11.

30. *Budget local du Tonkin, 1939* (Hanoi: Imprimerie Le Van Tan, 1938) and *Budget local de l'Annam, 1939* (Hue: Imp. Dac Lap, 1939).

31. *Budget Général: Compte administratif, Exercice 1938* (Hanoi: IDEO, 1938).

32. *Les Paysans du Delta Tonkinois,* op. cit.

33. For the moment, we leave out of consideration the important trade in human labour power which will be dealt with in the next section.

34. The volume of entries into Haiphong from coastal shipping was higher than the total tonnage (216 139) carried in French and foreign ships into the port.

35. The volume of exports in French and foreign shipping for 1936 was 912 412 tonnes compared with 112 791 tonnes in the coastal trade.

36. 1352 tonnes of rice and paddy, excluding broken rice and flour, were shipped to all regions in 1922 – equivalent to 0.14% of total rice and paddy exported from Saigon that year.

37. Robequain, op. cit., p. 281.

38. Nguyen Tien Hung, op. cit., pp. 26–8.

39. Le Chau, op. cit., p. 58.

40. *Rapports au Grand Conseil,* 1938, p. 104.

41. Robequain, op. cit., p. 96.

42. Octave Depuy, *Étude Comparative sur la Culture de l'*Hevea Brasiliensis *en Cochinchine et dans les divers pays du Moyen-Orient* (Paris, 1912) p. 26.

43. Statistique Générale de l'Indochine, *L'Evolution de l'Économie indochi-*

noise en 1948, supplément au Bulletin Économique de l'Indochine (Saigon, 1949) pp. 36–37. Note that no mention is made here of the Haiphong-Yunnan line which was privately run.

44. *Rapports au Grand Conseil* (Hanoi: Imprimerie G. Taupin, 1938) p. 364.

45. *L'Evolution de l'Économie indochinoise en 1947*, supplément au *Bulletin Économique de l'Indochine* (Saigon: Statistique Générale de l'Indochine, 1948) p. 27.

46. Andrus, op. cit., p. 88.

47. *Rapports au Grand Conseil*, 1938, p. 364.

48. Gouvernement Général de l'Indochine, Conseiller aux Affaires Économiques, No. 119. At the time, road repair was made constantly difficult by guerrilla attacks on material and equipment in all the main economic areas of Vietnam, *L'Evolution de l'Économie indochinoise en 1948* (Saigon, 1949) p. 36.

49. Population densities in the main rubber growing provinces of Gia Dinh, Thu Dau Mot and Bien Hoa were, in inhabitants per square kilometre, 160, 22 and 15 respectively. This compares with 704 and 676 per km^2 in Nam Dinh and Thai Binh provinces of the Red River delta. Murray, op. cit., pp. 270, 571.

50. *Rapports au Grand Conseil*, 1930, p. 166.

51. Due to the opening of the Trans Indo-China railway. *Rapports au Grand Conseil*, 1938, p. 104; see also the 1936 edition, p. 76.

52. *L'Evolution de l'Économie indochinoise en 1947*, op.cit., p. 12.

53. Murray, op. cit., p. 223.

54. The French plantation companies boasted that free food rations and health care constituted an important component of the wages of their labourers, whenever they were challenged about the low cash component. However, their generosity did not extend to cases of serious illness. Many of the workers suffered from malaria, which was then endemic to the highland areas, and these were packed off home, often arriving, at the end of their long and uncomfortable sea voyage, in a truly wretched state and without means of support. These cases became the occasion for political agitation against the whole contract labour system and forced the colonial government to intervene to control the traffic. A compulsory savings plan (*pécule*) was introduced to ensure that workers had sufficient funds upon their return and contractors were forced to ensure return to place of origin rather than point of embarkation. Hospitalisation was provided at Haiphong. I do not know how effective these measures were. See *Rapports au Grand Conseil*, 1930, p. 171; also Fonds des Amiraux, no. 64047, extract from M. Tupinier, Inspecteur lère classe des colonies, 'Rapport d'Inspection des Colonies', 30 January 1937, on below-subsistence wages of rubber plantation 'coolies' and the tiny contribution of payments in kind. M. Tupinier calculated that food alone would absorb the entire wage of a labourer and, unless his wife also earned money, clothing and other expenses would not be covered (lodging, of a kind, was provided free).

55. Robequain, op. cit., p. 207.

56. Murray, op. cit., p. 262.

57. See the letter from the President of the Société des Terres Rouges to the

Governor General in Hanoi, 20 April 1928, Fonds des Amiraux, No. 46443, which complains of a labour deficiency of about 15 per cent of requirements.

58. *Rapports au Grand Conseil,* 1930, pp. 171, 176.
59. Gourou showed that there were large-scale traditional migrations of wage labour to areas where the harvest came earlier by peasants who would then return to their own meagre plot of land when their own harvest became due. Op. cit., pp. 222–3.
60. *Rapports au Grand Conseil,* 1930.
61. Ibid., p. 176.
62. Ngo Vinh Long, op. cit.
63. For example, Thompson, op. cit.; Murray, op. cit. Evidence can also be found in the French archives. Anthony Grey based his reasonably accurate portrayal of conditions in the plantations in his novel, *Saigon,* on archive material.
64. *Rapports au Grand Conseil,* 1930, p. 177.
65. Thompson, op. cit., p. 155.
66. Tappers required a few weeks of training.
67. Fonds des Amiraux, No. 2772.
68. *Rapports au Grand Conseil,* 1930, p. 185.
69. Thompson, op. cit., p. 159.
70. *Rapports au Grand Conseil,* 1930, p. 171.
71. Ibid., p. 186.
72. Ibid. See also the 'Rapport' of M. Tupinier, op. cit.

Chapter Three   Economy of the Republic of Vietnam, 1955–75

1. President Eisenhower, in his memoirs, wrote that 'It was generally conceded that had an election been held, Ho Chi Minh would have been elected Premier', cited in G. Kolko, *The Roots of American Foreign Policy* (Boston: Beacon Press, 1969) p. 108.
2. 'Only the US presence after 1954 held the South together under far more favourable circumstances [than at the time of writing], and enabled Diem to refuse to go through with the 1954 provision calling for nationwide "free" elections in 1956. Even talking about a US withdrawal would undermine any chance of keeping a non-Communist government in South Vietnam.' *Declassified Documents Reference System* (*DDRS*) (Arlington (Va.): Carrollton Press, (78) 148A) p. 6. See also *The Pentagon Papers,* (*New York Times* edn) (London: Routledge & Kegan Paul, 1971) p. 26.
3. 'The loss of South Vietnam would make pointless any further discussion about the importance of Southeast Asia to the free world; we would have to face the near certainty that the remainder of Southeast Asia and Indonesia would move to a complete accommodation with Communism.' Memorandum from Rusk and McNamara to President Kennedy (*Pentagon Papers,* 11 November 1961, p. 155). See also Kolko, op.cit., pp. 105, 113.
4. The development of this system in the first three decades after the Second

World War has been extensively documented by, among others, Noam Chomsky, *American Power and the New Mandarins,* (Harmondsworth: Penguin, 1969) and *At War With Asia* (London: Fontana, 1971); G. Kolko, op. cit; D. Horowitz, *From Yalta to Vietnam* (Harmondsworth: Penguin, 1969); H. Magdoff, *The Age of Imperialism* (New York: Monthly Review Press, 1969); Peter Wiley, 'Vietnam and the Pacific Rim Strategy', *Leviathan,* vol. 1, no. 3, June 1969; S. Hymer, *The Multinational Corporation: A Radical Approach* (Cambridge University Press, 1979).

5. Five per cent per annum in real terms (at 1960 constant prices) according to *Tinh Hinh Kinh Te Mien Nam 1955–1975 (THKTMN)* (Economic Situation in the Southern Region 1955–1975) (Ho Chi Minh City: Institute for Social Sciences, 1979) p. 114.

6. J. Race, *War Comes to Long An* (Berkeley: University of California Press, 1972) pp. 56–60; Nguyen Kien, *Le Sud-Vietnam depuis Dien Bien Phu* (Paris: Maspero, 1963) pp. 126–7; Robert Scigliano, *South Vietnam: Nation Under Stress* (Boston: Houghton Mifflin, 1964) pp. 121–2.

7. Clive Hamilton, 'Industrialisation in the "Four Little Tigers" of East Asia', in P. Limqueco and B. McFarlane (eds) *Neo-Marxist Theories of Development* (London: Croom Helm, 1983) p. 154.

8. F. C. Child, *Essays on Economic Growth, Capital Formation and Public Policy in Vietnam* (Saigon: Michigan State University Vietnam Advisory Group, 1961); Milton C. Taylor, 'South Vietnam: Lavish Aid, Limited Progress', *Pacific Affairs,* vol. XXXIV, (Fall 1961) no. 3; Lloyd D. Musolf, 'Public Enterprise and Development Perspectives in South Vietnam', *Asian Survey,* vol. III, (August 1963) no. 8, pp. 368–70; State Dept, Cable from US Embassy Saigon, 23 December 1963, *DDRS,* (76) 131D. State Department officials complained in 1959 that the government of South Vietnam 'continues to regard economic improvements as feasible and desirable only to the extent that they do not detract from current defence strength' and that it had no long range priority of modernisation. Intelligence Report No. 8008, 5 May 1959, *DDRS,* (77) 77C.

9. Op. cit., pp. 362–70.

10. CIA 'The Situation in South Vietnam', 20–24 March 1964, *DDRS,* (77) 177C. Centrally controlled distribution systems had also been a method used in South Korea for extracting agricultural surpluses and subsidising industrial development. See Hamilton, op. cit., p. 155.

11. Race, op. cit., ch. 3, especially p. 110; Kolko, op.cit., p. 117; *An Outline History of the Vietnam Workers' Party,* 2nd edn (Hanoi: FLPH, 1978) pp. 100–2.

12. *Pentagon Papers,* pp. 166–238.

13. Child, op. cit., p. 135; National Security Council, 'Progress Report, March 14, 1957' *DDRS,* (78) 389A; reports cited in Gordon White, 'Political Economy of Vietnamisation', *Eastern Horizon,* vol. 11, (1972) no. 2, pp. 53–4. For more general criticisms of the bureaucratic inadequacies of the regime, the tendency to look after personal or group interests, the military, religious and regional factionalism which provided obstacles to development, see CIA, National Intelligence Estimate no. 53–66, 15 December 1966, *DDRS,* (76) 150A.

14. They overstate the importance of this. Informal capital markets can work just as well. The complaint is really about the failure of capital markets to channel funds in the direction desired.

15. Business International Asia/Pacific Ltd., *Risks and Rewards in Vietnam's Markets* (Hong Kong, 1974) p. 33. Cf. the policy followed in both Malaysia and Indonesia today of favouring ethnic Malay over local Chinese entrepreneurs. A similar policy was pursued in Thailand during the 1950s.

16. 8.5 per cent of the plantation area of Vietnam (whole country) was owned by Vietnamese towards the end of French rule, although many of these were in fact naturalised French citizens. See T. Hodgkin, *Vietnam: The Revolutionary Path* (London: Macmillan, 1981) p. 182.

17. In 1956, of 2768 enterprises, 23 per cent (633) were foreign-owned, but these represented 97 per cent of the capital value (*THKTMN*, p. 53). In 1938 the French had owned 95 per cent of the European capital invested in business enterprises and all the capital invested in government securities (J. Buttinger, *Vietnam: A Dragon Embattled* (New York: Praeger, 1967) p. 187).

18. 'Vietnam and the Implementation of the United States Economic and Military Assistance Program', *DDRS* (R) 248F, p. 30. For a description of the social class structure of Vietnam and the role of different ethnic groups under the French, see Buttinger, op. cit., pp. 161–2, 194, 196: 'The controlling positions in the capitalist sector of the economy were held by the French, and to a minor degree by the Chinese; only at its fringe did the Vietnamese middle class, with a small percentage of total investments, participate in the development of capitalism in their own country.'

19. Child, op. cit., pp. 87, 112–3.

20. Ibid., pp. 157–8. See also Musolf, op. cit., on the concentration and centralisation of ownership of resources in ethnic Vietnamese hands.

21. A CIA report in 1970 echoed the lament of earlier years in asserting that the bulk of South Vietnamese leaders 'lack any basic sensitivity to the problems of rural people or dedication to their welfare' (a charge which may also be levelled at the Americans themselves: see note 4 above), CIA, 17 April 1970, pp. 7, 9, *DDRS*, (77) 270C.

22. Chi Do Pham, *Inflationary Finance in Wartime South Vietnam: 1960–72* (University of Pennsylvania, PhD thesis, 1976) p. 126; Asian Development Bank, *Southeast Asia's Economy in the 1970s* (London: Longman, 1971) pp. 595–8; see also US Embassy Saigon to State Dept, 7 October 1963, *DDRS*, (R) 828A.

23. US Department of Defense, April 1966, *DDRS*, (80) 249E.

24. Promulgated in March 1970. The main provisions were for accelerated distribution of land appropriated from large holders and former French *colons* under Ordinance 57 of 1956 by Diem, and to recognise the right to occupancy of farmers who had received land under various Viet Minh or National Liberation Front reforms. CIA Intelligence Report, 10 July 1967, *DDRS*, (R) 49E.

25. Industrial Development Bank of Vietnam, *Industrial Development News*, Saigon, March 1974; Dale L. Moody *The Manufacturing Sector in the*

Republic of Vietnam: its Structure, Productivity and Development (University of Florida, PhD thesis, 1975) pp. 132–3 (see also Moody's criticisms of these measures on pp. 133–4. These are chiefly based on lack of consistency of investment criteria and lack of clear priorities between them); Business International Asia/Pacific, op. cit., p. 30; National Bank of Vietnam, *Economic Bulletin,* Saigon, (1974) no. 11–12, pp. 74ff.

26.   No data are available giving a sectoral breakdown of investment. Using the data on GDP by sector and Gross Capital Formation in constant 1960 prices of the National Institute of Statistics, there would appear to be a stronger relationship between total investment effort and output in the tertiary sector than between total investment and output in agriculture (see *THKTMN,* pp. 114—8). But these data are not considered as reliable as those of the National Bank (in current prices only). In particular, the use of constant prices would appear to have distorted the size of investment relative to GDP.

27.   E.g. National Bank of Vietnam, *Economic Bulletin,* Saigon (1974), no. 11–12, where citizens are urged to lead a 'simple and economical life'.

28.   See Figure 3.3. A major cause of disruption to agricultural production was the displacement of large numbers of people (at least 5.8 million according to World Bank, *Current Economic Position and Prospects of the Republic of Vietnam,* Report No. 315-VN, 18 January 1974, p. 1), many of whom contributed to the rapid and socially disruptive expansion of urban areas. Other long-term problems were caused by neglect of irrigation, drainage, flood control and salinity prevention systems (World Bank, *The Socialist Republic of Vietnam, An Introductory Economic Report,* Report no. 1718-VN, 12 August 1977, p. 49).

29.   Exports of rice fell from an average of 213 000 tonnes per annum in 1958–60 ($US 21.4 million p.a.) to zero in 1965. Rubber exports fell from an average 72 000 t ($US 43.5 million) per annum in 1958–60 to 26 000 t ($US 8.3 million) per annum in 1971–73. *THKTMN,* pp. 43—4, 136, 138.

30.   Income from inherited or donated property, bank deposits, government bonds and pensions was exempt. Alimony was tax deductible (Business International Asia/Pacific, op. cit., p. 108). Personal and company tax accounted for an average of 6–7 per cent of domestic revenue, or less than three per cent of total revenue (Chi Do Pham, op. cit., p. 105).

31.   Ibid. These included, for example, customs duties and austerity taxes on luxury consumer goods.

32.   Calculated from ibid., p. 31, and *THKTMN,* p. 75.

33.   Chi Do Pham, op. cit., p. 5.

34.   Ibid., p. 7.

35.   Chi Do Pham also suggests that uncertainty brought about by war conditions caused people to hold cash balances rather than goods (for precautionary motive), op. cit., pp. 150–1.

36.   *THKTMN,* p. 75.

37.   Ibid., p. 113. This also contributed to lack of capital formation in the public sector without leading to a high rate of private capital formation.

38.   Economist Intelligence Unit, *Quarterly Economic Review: Indochina,* (1971) no. 4, p. 4; US Embassy Saigon to State Dept, 18 November 1961,

on the withdrawal as a result of public outcry, of a bill before the
National Assembly to reduce salaries of officials in an effort to reduce
the deficit (*DDRS,* (R) 809D).

39.   The director of the state sugar corporation turned out to be a member of
      the NLF who was subsequently Minister of Justice in the Provisional
      Revolutionary Government until mid-1976 (see *Far Eastern Economic
      Review* (FEER) 12 June 1986, p. 52). Shares in some of the more
      profitable public enterprises were later offered to holders of Land
      Reform Bonds, but the offer was infrequently taken up (see Musolf, op.
      cit., p. 369).

40.   Child, op. cit., p. 8.

41.   Ibid., pp. 10–13.

42.   Ibid., pp. 16–17. These foreign exchange reserves accumulated because
      the level of US aid under the Commercial Import Program was at that
      time (1961) fixed according to the size of the domestic, rather than the
      external, deficit – the former consistently exceeding the latter. The ratio-
      nale behind the policy was to encourage deficit financing of the war. See
      US Embassy Saigon to State Dept, 28 May 1963, *DDRS,* (R) 820C.

43.   Child, op. cit., p. 77.

44.   For a detailed examination of these two cases see Hamilton, op. cit.

45.   See Robert L. Sansom, *The Economics of Insurgency in the Mekong
      Delta of Vietnam* (Cambridge (Mass.): MIT Press, 1970).

46.   S. Kuznets, 'International Differences in Capital Formation and Financ-
      ing', in Universities – National Bureau Committee of Economic Re-
      search, *Capital Formation and Economic Growth* (Princeton University
      Press, 1955) p. 23.

47.   *THKTMN,* p. 215–6 gives two estimates of population based on
      different assumptions. (The official RVN estimates give a 1975 total
      which is too low and the estimate of the Institute of Social Science based
      on the 1976 census and an assumed growth rate of 2.6 per cent, produces
      an estimate for 1956 which is probably too high.) For the purposes of
      this chapter I have calculated an alternative series based on an estimated
      population of 12.6 million in 1956 and the census result of 23.6 million in
      1976.

48.   However, B. Fall (*The Two Vietnams,* London: Pall Mall Press, 1963, p.
      307) cites a South Vietnamese government view that the construction of
      strategic hamlets and other war-related activities at this time would lead
      to economic expansion. Given widespread peasant resistance to the
      wholesale population movement involved, it seems an unlikely possi-
      bility.

49.   See, for example, US Information Agency, February 1965, *DDRS,* (75)
      895A; CIA. 17–23 June 1965, *DDRS,* (75) 354A. According to CIA
      Intelligence Memorandum, 29 June 1965, *DDRS,* (76) 231D, only 30 per
      cent of the population were in areas 'now considered pacified'. At the
      time of the December 1964 coup d'état which brought Air Vice-Marshal
      Ky and General Thieu to power, Thieu thought that 'the Communists
      controlled seventy-five percent of the countryside. We controlled only
      the chief towns. We had the impression we would be overrun.' Cited by
      Michael Maclear, *Vietnam: The Ten Thousand Day War* (London:

Thames Methuen, 1981), p. 176. For discussion of the economy of the Communist-controlled areas and the likely effects on both actual performance of the economy and official Saigon reporting of it, see Chapter 4.

50. Reasons given for the inflation were cumulative impact of US troop expenditures, shortages of skilled manpower, port congestion creating difficulties in aid distribution and shortages of rice supplies for urban areas. See CIA 10 July 1967, *DDRS,* (R) 49E; State Department, Southeast Asia Program, December 1968, *DDRS,* (75) 9B; CIA, 19 January 1966, *DDRS,* (78) 345A: National Security Council, Agenda Papers 9 May 1966, *DDRS,* (78) 63A.

51. See World Bank (1974) op. cit., p. 49. The troop withdrawals began in 1969 and were completed by 1973. Piastre purchases by the US disbursing officer in selected years were as follows (in $US million): 1964, 42.0; 1966, 233.1; 1968, 310.8; 1971, 403.1; 1973, 100.0. Chi Do Pham, op. cit., p. 73 and World Bank (1974) op. cit., p. 24.

52. Cited in Moody, op. cit., p. 59. See also Asian Development Bank, op. cit., p. 618, for similar estimates of the net US aid contribution.

53. See Frank Snepp, *Decent Interval,* (London: Allen Lane, 1980) pp. 54–6. At the end of 1971 only 3 per cent of the South's population was officially considered to be in 'contested' areas (Maclear, op. cit., p. 353). By the time of the Paris Peace Accords, however, the Communist controlled areas would appear to have expanded somewhat – see Snepp, map on p. 55.

54. Some damage to productive capacity did occur, especially in textiles, during the Tet offensive and this is reflected in production statistics (see next section). One estimate of damage within the Saigon area as a result of this offensive, puts the value of industrial capacity destroyed at $US50 million (State Dept, Southeast Asia Program, December 1968, *DDRS,* (75) 9B. An index of industrial production compiled from National Bank sources, shows industrial production at the end of 1974 as below the 1965 level (*THKTMN*, p. 177).

55. *THKTMN*, pp. 116–18. The division into 'productive' and 'unproductive' (or services) sectors is in accordance with socialist practice. While there are many conceptual problems with this type of categorisation, it is useful for our purposes to separate the main sectors in which increasing output and productivity would be expected to underpin the development of an industrial economy. The figures here should be used with caution as there are some unexplained discrepancies in the original data. However, they may be useful as an indication of trends.

56. M. Trued, 'South Vietnam's Industrial Development Center', *Pacific Affairs,* vol. XXXIII (September 1960) no. 3, says that the eleven commercial banks in South Vietnam 'almost entirely confine themselves to financing the export-import trade, only rarely providing funds for longer-term investment by renewing short-term advances. Moreover, such longer-term loans were usually in construction and real estate.' (p. 255) In 1974 the commercial banks provided only one per cent of total loans made to agriculture, farmers having to rely mainly on village merchants and money lenders or family sources. The Government's

Agricultural Development Bank provided less than 15 per cent of loans (World Bank (1974) op. cit., p. 44).

57.   See, for example, Asian Development Bank, op. cit., p. 595. Taylor, op. cit., points out that between 1955 and 1960 only 13 per cent of US aid went to economic and technical projects and within this 45 per cent went to highway development and only 9 per cent to agriculture (p. 253). Other aid projects included such things as a broadcasting station for the Presidential Palace and technical assistance for fingerprinting the population (p. 252).

58.   Asian Development, Bank, op. cit., p. 598. This accusation also came from the NLF: 'The policy adopted by the US AID Agency is not favourable for rice production in South Vietnam because the United States has become an important rice-exporting country', in 'Vietnamization – the Path Leading to Collapse' (captured NLF document), published in *Vietnam: Documents and Research Notes,* no. 74, (Saigon: US AID Mission in Vietnam, February 1970) pp. 22–3. This document goes on to accuse the United States of dumping goods on the Saigon market.

59.   US Embassy Bangkok to State Dept, 10 July 1965, *DDRS,* (R) 7481. Under PL480 arrangements the US Government buys farm produce from farmers, which is then donated or resold under aid programmes.

60.   National Institute of Statistics, *Tinh Hinh Kinh Te Viet Nam 1971* (Economic Situation of Vietnam 1971) (Saigon, 1972) p. 44.

61.   *THKTMN,* pp. 117–118. These figures are from National Bank, Saigon, sources. An alternative set of data from the National Institute of Statistics, in current prices, suggests an even larger shift towards the services sector over the same period (from 44 to 52 per cent) – see NIS, *Statistical Yearbook* (Saigon, 1969, 1972). The share of agriculture in South Vietnam was lower than in neighbouring countries in the late 1960s (Cambodia 56%, Indonesia 62%, West Malaysia 46%, Philippines 51%, Thailand 50%). Asian Development Bank, op. cit., pp. 113, 192.

62.   Rubber yields per hectare fell from 0.93 tonnes in 1956 to 0.24 tonnes in 1972. *THKTMN,* p. 138.

63.   CIA 17–23 June 1965, *DDRS,* (75) 354A; National Bank of Vietnam, *Annual Report,* Saigon, 1968, p. 22. Production was also affected by competition from synthetics. Fall, op.cit., points out that even if replanting had proceeded as planned in the early 1960s, rubber production could not have recovered before the early 1970s. Buttinger, op. cit., p. 536, says that acceleration of production in the 1960s occurred at the expense of the rehabilitation of the rubber trees.

64.   *THKTMN,* pp. 43–5. See also note 30 above. Rubber provided 57 per cent of all export income in the period 1955–74.

65.   Moody, op. cit., pp. 100–1.

66.   Exports of rice ceased altogether after 1964. Imports were 130 000 tonnes in 1965 and then averaged 555 000 tonnes a year from 1966 to 1970 before dropping to 250 000 tonnes a year in 1971–4. *THKTMN,* pp. 40, 136.

67.   US rice exports to Vietnam as a percentage of total US rice exports rose from 2.2 per cent in 1964 to an average of 38 per cent in 1966–72. US

Department of Agriculture, *Agricultural Statistics* (Washington: 1971, 1974. US Government Printing Office). As a rough guide, a scatter diagram based on figures from the same source shows quite a strong relationship between US rice production levels and exports of rice to Vietnam in the previous year.

68. The aims of the land reform were both political (allegiance of the peasantry) and economic (to obtain an increased agricultural surplus), CIA, *DDRS,* (R) 49E. Fall, op. cit., p. 294, gives 1938 paddy production as 5.3 million tonnes. While this figure was occasionally reached in the early 1960s, it was not decisively passed until the 1970s.

69. Chi Do Pham, op. cit., p. 5; Gordon White, op. cit., pp. 51, 53. The exception to this was Thieu's disastrous 'rice war' in late 1973 which forced peasants to sell rice at artificially low prices in an effort to prop up falling real wages of troops and city dwellers. The result was simply a drying up of marketed rice surpluses (Gabriel Kolko, *Vietnam: Anatomy of a War 1940–1975,* (London, Allen & Unwin, 1986) p. 493).

70. CIA, 22 July 1968, *DDRS,* (R) 50A; 10 July 1967, *DDRS,* (R) 49E; US Embassy Saigon to State Dept, 7 November 1961, *DDRS,* (R) 802F. For the post-1975 period see Chapter 4.

71. Exports of wood products increased dramatically in the final years of the regime, rising from zero before 1973 to $US11.9 million in 1973 and $US10.7 million in 1974 (or 19.6 and 14.3 per cent of total export income in those years). See *THKTMN,* p. 44.

72. Figures for charcoal production should be treated with extra caution since the main producing area, Ca Mau province, was an NLF stronghold – US Embassy Saigon to State Dept, 22 November 1961, *DDRS,* (R) 811E. Average annual imports of petroleum products increased from $US17.4 million in 1957–64 to $US30 million in 1965–71 and $US75.6 million in 1972 – *THKTMN,* pp. 39–40.

73. The industry suffered a slowdown in growth, however, during the early 1970s when the mechanised fishing fleet was affected by oil price increases and between 1978–80 when much of the modern fishing fleet was used for illegal emigration. See *Industrial Development News* (Saigon: Industrial Development Bank of Vietnam, March 1974), and International Monetary Fund, *Socialist Republic of Vietnam – Recent Economic Developments,* 18 May 1982, p. 6.

74. Moody, op. cit., p. 87. Over 60 per cent of *all* industry was located in Saigon according to the World Bank, 1974, op. cit., p. 49.

75. Ibid., p. 94.

76. Ibid., p. 92.

77. In 20 out of 28 industries in Moody's study, seven or less firms sold over 80 per cent of the industry's output and in nearly all cases these firms accounted for more than 50 per cent of employment in that industry. 'However, in only 7 industries did these firms account for more than 50 per cent of enterprises.' Ibid., p. 94.

78. There are discrepancies in the data – see Table 3.2.

79. Ibid., pp. 100–1. The tendency was for the share of imported raw materials to rise over the period 1962–8.

80. Business International Asia/Pacific, op. cit., p. 26.

81. In May 1975 Vietnam was added to country Group Z in the US export control classification which imposes a general trade embargo. The US have also made efforts to prevent multilateral aid agencies lending to Vietnam since 1975 — see *Far Eastern Economic Review,* 9 May 1980, 19 September 1980, 1 May 1981, 10 July 1981. For a discussion of US foreign policy in the region during the aftermath of the Vietnam War, see M. Beresford, R. Catley and F. Pilkington, 'America's New Pacific Rim Strategy', *Journal of Contemporary Asia,* vol. 9 (1979) no. 1.

82. Industries in which locally produced raw materials were already used extensively included salt, fish sauce, rice milling, furniture, ceramics, cement, rubber articles, hides and tanning, footwear and hats, printing, glass – Moody, op. cit., p. 101.

83. National Bank of Vietnam, *Annual Report,* 1968, Saigon, p. 29; World Bank (1974), op. cit., p. 53.

84. *THKTMN,* p. 71.

85. According to World Bank (1974), op. cit., p. 56, there were 83 000 trucks and 61 000 cars in 1972. *THKTMN,* p. 180 gives figures for cars: 1960, 37 600 and 1972, 61 700; and heavy vehicles: 1960, 19 300 and 1972, 79 400. Business International Asia/Pacific, op. cit., p. 79 says that at the end of 1971 there were 170 000 trucks and buses in service. Whatever the real number, W. Duiker, *Vietnam Since the Fall of Saigon* (Athens, Ohio: Ohio University Centre for International Studies, 1980) p. 31, cites a 1977 report that nearly a third of all trucks in Vietnam (North and South) were out of operation through lack of spare parts.

86. CIA, 29 June 1965, p. 7, *DDRS,* (76) 231D.

87. See, for example, CIA, 6 January 1965, *DDRS,* (75) 133A; 17–23 June 1965, *DDRS,* (75) 354A; National Security Council, Agenda Papers, 9 May 1966, *DDRS,* (78) 63A; W. Duiker, op. cit., p. 31.

88. Business International Asia/Pacific, op. cit., p. 78.

89. World Bank, 1974, op. cit., p. 57. That many bridges destroyed during the war have not been fully repaired was confirmed by officials in Ben Tre province during my visit there in October 1985.

90. Ibid.

91. Ibid., pp. 56–7.

92. Only about a dozen of the southern region's 61 locomotives were in service in 1982 according to a UNDP report cited in *FEER,* 21 May 1982, p. 16. See also, Citibank, *Vietnam: An Economic Study* (Hong Kong, 1976) p. 46.

93. World Bank (1974), op. cit., p. 54.

94. Ibid.

95. *FEER,* 9 May 1980, p. 50.

96. See World Bank (1974), op. cit., p. 50. CIA, 'The Situation in South Vietnam', 17–23 June 1965, *DDRS,* (75) 354A; see also National Security Council, Agenda Papers, 9 May 1966, *DDRS,* (78) 63A.

97. *THKTMN,* p. 110.

98. Chris Nyland, 'Vietnam, the Plan/Market Contradiction and the Transition to Socialism', *Journal of Contemporary Asia,* vol. 11 (1981) no. 4, p. 438 (among others) cites official post-war estimates of the numbers of

prostitutes (500 000) and heroin users (300 000) among the Southern population.

99. *THKTMN*, p.110. Of these, 15 per cent were in the armed forces and the other four per cent in civilian public services (World Bank (1974), op. cit., p. 1).

100. *THKTMN*, p. 110. In 1966 commerce, banking and services accounted for 5 per cent, manufacturing 2.3 per cent, construction 2.6 per cent, transport 2.3 per cent, public utilities 0.6 per cent. The more detailed breakdown is not available for later years.

101. Ibid., p. 113.

102. Ibid.

103. 710 000 in the regular army alone in 1973 (*THKTMN*, p. 73).

104. 19.7 per cent as against 20.6 per cent for urban areas (ibid., p. 113).

105. See Sansom's study of two villages in Dinh Tuong province, op. cit.

106. *THKTMN*, p. 33. From 1965–75 the ratio of exports to imports averaged 5.2 per cent compared with the 1956–64 average of 25.4 per cent.

107. International Monetary Fund, *International Financial Statistics*, various issues. This outflow was marginal and was offset by an inflow of direct investment capital in 1973 and 1974 (total $US11 million).

108. CORDS (Civil Operations and Rural Development Support), for example, was to combine counter-insurgency methods with a programme of public works in the countryside, to improve Government popularity following the failure of the Strategic Hamlets – see Snepp, op. cit., p. 25. But on the failure of this 'economic' approach see Maclear, op. cit, pp. 349–50.

109. Snepp, op. cit., pp. 96–9, also comments on the way in which corruption at high levels of the government sapped morale and contributed to defeat. But warnings of this were, he says, consistently and deliberately ignored by the American government. Snepp argues that public outcry in the South against corruption (led by a conservative Buddhist priest) contributed directly to Hanoi's decision to launch the final offensive.

110. Loans were a relatively minor source of foreign aid. In 1972 and 1973, for example, loans amounted to 3.5 per cent of total aid (World Bank (1974), op.cit., p. 32). In 1972, debt service payments to the US amounted to only $VN1.2 billion, or 1.4 per cent of export income for that year (*THKTMN*, p. 18). According to the World Bank, for the 12 years 1960–71, 42.5 per cent of the trade deficit was met by net invisible receipts (mainly piastre purchases) and 57.5 per cent by foreign aid in various forms (p. 24).

111. Calculated from data in Asian Development Bank, op. cit., pp. 617–8.

112. *THKTMN*, pp. 13, 16. However, this was still a decline in real terms and was insufficient to offset completely the decline in piastre purchases (World Bank (1974), op. cit., p. 24).

113. Average imports of nitrogenous fertiliser increased from 67 000 tonnes per annum in 1956–67, to 190 000 in 1968–73. Agricultural machinery imports also increased after 1968. *THKTMN*, p. 189. One estimate for the 1970s put the value of imported agricultural inputs at $US156

million a year, of which $100 million consisted of fertiliser (World Bank (1974) op. cit., p. iii). However, imported fertilisers did not necessarily reach the fields – see the comments of R. Komer, founder of CORDS, in Maclear, op. cit., p. 350.

114. BBC, *Summary of World Broadcasts*, FE/W870/A/37, 24 March 1976, mentions the existence of 18 fertiliser factories in the South only 12 months after the end of the war.

115. National Bank of Vietnam, *Bulletin économique*, No. 9–10, 1972. An increase in the United States' share of imports occurred mainly at the expense of Hong Kong, Japan, Taiwan and Thailand (Economist Intelligence Unit, *Quarterly Economic Review: Indochina,* (1971) no. 4, p. 4.

116. National Bank, op. cit.

117. Ibid., (1971) no. 11–12, p. 41; Business International Asia/Pacific, op. cit., p. 62.

118. Vietnam Council on Foreign Relations, *Vietnam Economic Report,* June 1971, p. 8; Business International Asia/Pacific, op. cit., p. 62.

119. Vietnam Council on Foreign Relations, *Vietnam Economic Report,* April 1971, p. 5.

120. See Musolf, op. cit., for details; also Business International Asia/Pacific, op. cit., p. 26.

121. See note 17 on foreign ownership of enterprises in 1956. In 1974 there were 274 firms with joint Vietnamese-foreign ownership and foreign capital represented 69 per cent of the total capital value of these firms (*THKTMN*, p. 53).

122. France ranked eleventh among contributors of foreign investment between 1963 and 1975, behind Japan, USA, South Korea, Switzerland, Taiwan, UK, Singapore, West Germany and Panama (Japan, USA and South Korea providing 59 per cent of the total). *THKTMN*, p. 61.

123. Altogether, $US10.6 million plus 0.7 million French francs, *THKTMN*, p. 61.

124. Only nine enterprises were capitalised at more than $VN500 million and of these, five were more than 90 per cent government-owned. A further 21 were capitalised at $VN100–500 million (Business International Asia/ Pacific, op. cit., p. 25).

125. See p. 70 on the concentration of output in these two industries. Ownership details are found in ibid., p. 28.

126. This approach is usually associated with Michal Kalecki. See his *Selected Essays on the Economic Growth of the Socialist and Mixed Economy* (Cambridge University Press, 1972).

127. The point is brought out very well in the model of L. G. Stolleru ('An Optimal Policy for Economic Growth', *Econometrica*, vol. 33, (1965) no. 2, April, applied to Algeria.

128. Nyland, op. cit., pp. 439–43; Duiker, op. cit., pp. 7–8; Bruce Grant (ed.), *The Boat People* (Melbourne: Penguin, 1979) for accounts of this instability.

129. Communist Party of Vietnam, *4th National Congress Documents* (Hanoi: FLPH, 1977). See also, P. Limqueco and B. McFarlane, 'Problems of Economic Planning for Underdeveloped Socialist Countries', *Journal of Contemporary Asia*, vol. 9, (1979) no. 1, p. 20.

Chapter Four Southern Agriculture

1. See Christine Pelzer White, 'Debates in Vietnamese Development Policy', *IDS Discussion Paper,* (Brighton: University of Sussex, 1982).
2. *Translations on Vietnam,* no. 1916, JPRS, 68992, p. 134.
3. *Translations on Vietnam,* no. 1983, JPRS, 70036, p. 10.
4. *So Lieu Thong Ke,* 1979, p. 37; 1980, p. 41. See also, G. Nguyen Tien Hung, *Economic Development of Socialist Vietnam 1955–80* (New York: Praeger, 1977) p. 108.
5. *Far Eastern Economic Review,* 29 January 1982.
6. See Chapters 5 and 6.
7. In 1979 the nutritional density (persons per hectare of land cultivated with staple food crops) for the different regions was as follows: (i) for the three central provinces of the Red River delta (Hai Hung, Thai Binh, Ha Nam Ninh) 8.0; (ii) for seven provinces of the central coast (Thanh Hoa, Nghe Tinh, Binh Tri Thien, Quang Nam-Da Nang, Nghia Binh, Phu Khanh, Thuan Hai) 7.8; (iii) for the nine provinces of the Mekong delta 5.4 (Long An 4.6, Dong Thap 5.6, Tien Giang 6.0, Ben Tre 7.5, Cuu Long 5.9, An Giang 5.5, Hau Giang, 5.1, Kien Giang 4.3, Minh Hai 4.7 – the last four being in the western part of the delta). Calculated from General Statistical Office, *So Lieu Thong Ke 1979* (Statistical Data), Hanoi, 1980, pp. 12–13, 56–7.
8. The Stanford Research Institute (*Land reform in Vietnam,* Menlo Park, Calif., 1968, Summary volume, p. 33) estimated the undeveloped arable area in 1965 as 20.2 per cent of the total land area, or nearly 3.5 million hectares (compared with the 1968 cultivated area of 2.3m ha). Nguyen Ngoc Triu, Minister of Agriculture of the SRV, estimated in 1980 that half a million hectares in the South has been abandoned and left untilled, sometimes for a dozen years; *Vietnam Report,* no. 2205, JPRS, 76196, p. 56.
9. Clearance of unexploded ordnance was done primarily by the army. According to one source, in the most heavily affected province of Binh Tri Thien (straddling the 17th parallel), eight million explosive devices were removed from 500 km^2 of arable land over a two-year period from 1975, at the cost of hundreds of lives. Nguyen Khac Vien, *Southern Vietnam 1975–1985,* (Hanoi: FLPH, 1985) p. 62.
10. According to Vietnamese sources, about 1.7 million hectares (10 per cent of the land area) of Southern Vietnam were affected by defoliants, including at least 12 per cent of forests and five per cent of agricultural land. *Herbicides and Defoliants in War: the Long Term Effects on Man and Nature,* (Hanoi: Vietnam Courier, 1983) p. 7.
11. This history is documented in, among others, Ngo Vinh Long, *Before the Revolution* (Cambridge Mass.: MIT Press, 1973), and Samuel L. Popkin, *The Rational Peasant* (Berkeley: University of California Press, 1979).
12. Irene Norlund, 'Rice Production in Colonial Vietnam 1900–1930', in I. Norlund, S. Cederroth and I. Gerdin (eds), *Rice Societies* (London and Riverdale: Curzon/Riverdale, 1986).
13. See, for example, Jeffrey Race, *War Comes to Long An,* (Berkeley: University of California Press, 1972).
14. Robert L. Sansom, *The Economics of Insurgency in the Mekong Delta of Vietnam* (Cambridge Mass.: MIT Press, 1970) pp. 57, 69.

15. US Defense Dept, Memorandum, 27 April 1961, *DDRS*, (78) 147A.
16. US Defense Dept, Memorandum 16 March 1964, *DDRS*, (78) 148A.
17. Cited in M. Maclear, *Vietnam: The Ten Thousand Day War*, (London: Thames Methuen, 1981) p. 176.
18. CIA Intelligence Memorandum, 29 June 1965, *DDRS*, (76) 231D.
19. Wilfred Burchett, *My Visit to the Liberated Zones of South Vietnam* (Hanoi: FLPH, 1966). The visit was made during 1964.
20. I do not mean to imply here that the chain of command was separate – the decision to launch all three offensives was taken by the Political Bureau of the Vietnam Workers' Party.
21. F. Snepp, *Decent Interval* (London: Allen Lane, 1980) p. 55.
22. R. Catley and B. McFarlane, 'The Vietnamese Social Model', *Australian Quarterly*, December 1974, p. 32. The material cited from this article is based on an interview by one of the authors with Ly Van Sau, a representative of the PRG at the Paris peace talks.
23. R. Sansom, op. cit.
24. 'Resolution on Economic and Financial Missions from the Present Time to Early 1969' (captured NLF document), *Vietnam Documents and Research Notes*. no. 49 (Saigon: US AID Mission to Vietnam, January 1969).
25. It seems that in spite of later efforts to increase the circulation of goods between the two zones, such taxation on movement of goods continued in some areas even after 1975. In December 1975 the PRG administration of Quang Nam Da Nang province issued a communiqué authorising the free circulation of goods within the province: 'Localities and sectors must not interdict and obstruct circulation of goods, nor must they stop and impose taxes on transport of goods. Checkpoints set up for communications control and taxation purposes must be dismantled except for security reasons.' BBC, *Summary of World Broadcasts (SWB)*, FE/W864/A/36, 11 February 1976.
26. CIA Intelligence Report, 15–21 April 1965, *DDRS*, (75) 240A. 'Resolution on Economic and Financial Missions . . .', (op. cit., pp. 10–11) says that tax rates are to be determined by 'patriotism, political enlightenment and economic and living conditions of the people.'
27. Catley and McFarlane, op. cit., pp. 32–3.
28. US Embassy Saigon to State Dept, 12 February 1964, *DDRS*, (75) 215E.
29. 'Resolution on Economic and Financial Missions . . .', op. cit., p. 15.
30. CIA Intelligence Report, 9 February 1964, *DDRS*, (78) 228A; 17–23 June 1965, *DDRS*, (75) 354A; 22 July 1968, *DDRS*, (R) 50A. By contrast, the armed forces of South Vietnam were 'unable, uninterested and ineffective in dealing with the rice collection problem' (CIA, 15 April 1965, *DDRS*, (75) 240A).
31. CIA Intelligence Memorandum, 29 June 1965, *DDRS* (76) 231D, p. 8.
32. Cited in Ngo Vinh Long, 'Agrarian Differentiation in the Southern Region of Vietnam', *Journal of Contemporary Asia*, vol. 14, (1983) no. 3, p. 287.
33. Gareth Porter, *Imperialism and Social Structure in Twentieth Century Vietnam*, PhD thesis, Cornell University, 1976.
34. J. M. Burr, *'Land-To-The-Tiller': Land Redistribution in South Vietnam 1970–73*, PhD thesis, University of Oregon, 1976, pp. 131, 225 et seq.

35. Tran Huu Quang, 'Nhan dien co cau gia cap o nong thon dong bang song Cuu Long' (Identifying class structure in the rural areas of the Mekong delta), *Nghien Cuu Kinh Te,* no. 128, August 1982, p. 32. The results of this survey and a second, much wider, survey carried out over the whole of Southern Vietnam during 1981 are similar. For data from the second see Ngo Vinh Long, 'Agrarian Differentiation . . .', op. cit., pp. 295–6.

36. C. Stuart Callison, ('The Land-To-The-Tiller Program and Rural Re-source Mobilisation in the Mekong Delta of South Vietnam', *Papers in International Studies,* Southeast Asia Series, no. 34, Athens, Ohio: Ohio University, 1974) found a significant increase in investment among recipients of Land-to-the-Tiller titles.

37. Sansom op. cit., pp. 124–5.

38. See Figure 3.3d for the decline in cattle and buffalo numbers after 1964. US troops deliberately shot buffaloes in villages which were suspected of sympathising with the NLF. See, among others, James W. Trullinger, *A Village at War* (Longman: New York and London, 1980) p. 117.

39. Sansom, op. cit., p. 215.

40. Le Nhat Quang, 'Mechanisation of Crop Growing in the Mekong Delta' *Nghien Cuu Kinh Te,* no. 115, June 1980, translated in JPRS 76711, *Vietnam Report* no. 2222, pp. 30–1. At the end of the war, An Giang province had 2000 tractors of over 30 hp, 1500 rototillers, 33 000 small water pumps, 1570 machines for stripping the leaves from rice ears, as well as a number of other types of machinery. See Tran Thanh Phuong, *Nhung Trang Ve An Giang* (Pages on An Giang) (Ho Chi Minh City: Van Nghe An Giang, 1984) p. 121.

41. Le Nhat Quang, op. cit., pp. 29, 32. This calculation was based on the existence of 133 700 hp of animal draught power and about 400 000 hp of mechanical draft power in the delta in 1978.

42. Imported fertilisers rose from an annual average of 96 000 tonnes per annum in 1955–62 to 207 000 in 1963–7 and 323 000 in 1968–73 (*THKTMN,* p. 189). For data on the area sown to HYV rice, see Burr op. cit., p. 177. The increase was from only 500 ha in 1967–8 to 835 000 ha in 1972–3.

43. Ibid., p. 30. The use of individually-owned pumps often led to disputes, however, as farmers using them to flush excess salinity or acidity from their soil merely dumped the problem on their neighbours' land.

44. *THKTMN,* p. 189.

45. According to data issued by the General Statistical Office, population density of the three central provinces of the Red River delta averaged 838 persons/km² in 1978 and 910 in 1984 (a growth-rate, affected by boundary changes, of 1.4 per cent per annum in the number of persons to each km²). Population densities in the Mekong delta ranged from 149/km² in Kien Giang to 526 in Tien Giang in 1978 and from 177 to 584 in the same two provinces in 1984. The number of persons per km² for the whole delta region grew at 3.5 per cent per annum between 1978 and 1984 (from 277 to 341/km²). Population densities of the central coastal provinces are much lower, but this is because they contain large tracts of sparsely populated highlands. General Statistical Office, *So Lieu Thong Ke, 1978,* p. 11; *1930–84,* pp. 7–8. Note, however, that an article

appearing in the October 1979 issue of the journal *Khoa Hoc Va Ky Thuat Nong Nghiep* (Agricultural Science and Technology) gave the population density of the Mekong delta in 1975 as only 187 persons per km^2 (JPRS 74937, *Vietnam Report* no. 2165, p. 55). The article would have been based on (pre-census) population estimates of the Thieu regime which apparently underestimated the size of the Southern population by about three million (*THKTMN*, p. 216). These earlier figures may also have led policy-makers into miscalculations about the availability of land for extensive development in the delta region.

46. NXL, 'The Readjustment of Land Holdings in Nam Bo', *Vietnam Courier*, vol. XIX, (1983) no. 1, January, p. 5.
47. Ngo Vinh Long, 'Agrarian Differentiation . . .', op. cit., p. 298.
48. See Communist Party of Vietnam, *4th National Congress Documents* (Hanoi: FLPH, 1977) p. 63.
49. The lack of precision is in the sources. *Nhan Dan* in January 1980 gave the number as 174, in April 1980 as 181 and in October 1980 as 176. The fluctuations are possibly due to new areas being opened up at the same time that others were abandoned – see JPRS 75301, 75637 and 76867, *Vietnam Report* no. 2177, p. 58, no. 2187, p. 37, no. 2230, p. 37. The number of state farms in the North by 1975 was 115, according to *Tap Chi Giang Vien* (Instructor's Review), No. 4, July-August 1979, p. 73.
50. *So Lieu Thong Ke 1930–1984*, (Hanoi: Tong Cuc Thong Ke, 1985) p. 114.
51. JPRS 75301, *Vietnam Report* no. 2177, p. 59.
52. JPRS 76867, *Vietnam Report* no. 2230 p. 38; also JPRS 75858, *Vietnam Report* no 2193, pp. 46–7, where, for example, rice yields in NEZ farms were put at under one tonne per hectare.
53. Thanh Dan, 'Some Opinions on Redistributing Agricultural Labour', *Khoa Hoc Va Ky Thuat Nong Nghiep*, (1979) no. 10, October, translated in JPRS 74937, *Vietnam Report* no. 2165, p. 58. This article asserted that the goal was to get ten million people to leave the northern deltas, although it contained no discussion of labour supply conditions of agriculture in those areas.
54. This I was told during a visit to Cu Chi district (rural area of Ho Chi Minh City) in December 1979.
55. Source: Dong Nai province, Ministry of Agriculture, October 1985.
56. An estimated $\frac{3}{4}$-million refugees, about one-half of them from Cambodia itself, added to the economic and social problems in the border areas.
57. Five years after the end of the war, about $\frac{3}{4}$-million people had left Ho Chi Minh City for the rural areas – either to the NEZs or to their villages of origin. According to officials I spoke to during December 1979, this was considered to be well below the government's target rate of departure. In fact, not many more would appear to have left during the next five years. In Hanoi, in October 1985, I was told by Ministry of Agriculture that a total of two million people had moved to the NEZs between 1976 and 1985 and that less than half of them came from the southern cities. See also note 53 above.
58. Data from Dong Nai Ministry of Agriculture. October 1985.

59. See, for example, *Nhan Dan*, 27 June 1978 (JPRS 71776, *Translations on Vietnam* no. 2058, p. 43) and 29 April 1980 (JPRS 75723, *Vietnam Report* no. 2189, p. 11).

60. M. Beresford, 'Vietnam: Northernizing the South or Southernizing the North?', *Contemporary Southeast Asia*, vol. 8 (1987) no. 3, p. 266.

61. JPRS 71776, *Translations on Vietnam* no. 2058 pp. 41–4.

62. A 1981 survey of the South showed that 2.5 per cent of farmers owned 58.5 per cent of tractor power over 25 hp, 50.5 per cent of rice mills and threshers, 52 per cent of sugar processing machinery and 'most' of the means of transport (Ngo Vinh Long, 'Agrarian Differentiation . . .', op. cit., p. 296).

63. Note that much more conflict in North Vietnam arose over the initial Land Reform in which large landlords and rich peasants had their land expropriated, than over the implementation of collectivisation policy.

64. JPRS 71599, *Translations on Vietnam* no. 2050, p. 47. In Vung Liem district (the 'key rice area of Cuu Long province'), only 34 per cent of surplus rice was purchased in 1977 and this amount was only 50 per cent of the amount bought in 1976. During the first three months of 1978, the district purchased 1719 tonnes, a fall of 3000 tonnes compared with the same period in 1977 (*Nhan Dan*, 9 June 1978, translated in JPRS, 71654, *Translations on Vietnam* no. 2052, p. 22). In An Giang province, only seven percent of output was purchased in 1977 and between 1977 and 1978 procurement from the 10th month crop fell from 23 000 tonnes to 6063 tonnes (*Nhan Dan*, 10 May 1978, translated in JPRS 71599, *Translations on Vietnam* no. 2050, pp. 39–40).

65. *Tap Chi Thong Ke*, no. 3, 1983, p. 47. See Ngo Vinh Long, 'Agrarian Differentiation . . .' op. cit., p. 287, for a pre-1975 estimate.

66. Cited in White, op. cit., p. 19.

67. For example, Chris Nyland, 'Vietnam, the Plan/Market Contradiction and the Transition to Socialism', *Journal of Contemporary Asia*, vol. 11 (1981). no. 4.

68. *Tap Chi Thong Ke*, no. 3, 1983, p. 47.

69. There were, however, some important gains in secondary food and industrial crop production in the South in 1976-9, especially the fairly consistent increases in output of maize, cassava, soybeans and tobacco.

70. *Far Eastern Economic Review*, 10 February 1983.

71. Tran Thanh Phuong, *Nhung Trang Ve An Giang* (Ho Chi Minh City: Van Nghe An Giang, 1984), p. 143.

72. See for example, BBC, *SWB*, FE/W1268/A/26, 4 January 1984; FE/W1271/A/23, 25 January 1984; FE/W1288/A/17, 23 May 1984; FE/W1289/A/15, 30 May 1984; FE/W1333/A/27, 10 April 1985.

73. See, for example, *Far Eastern Economic Review*, 10 April 1986.

74. Truong Chinh, 'Political Report', 6th Party Congress, *SWB*, FE/8447, 20 December 1986.

75. See BBC, *SWB*, FE/W1344/A/21, 26 June 1985.

76. *SWB*, FE/W1342/A/21, 12 June 1985.

77. This was apparent from my interviews. See also *SWB*, FE/W1372/A/39, 15 January 1986 for some data on Cuu Long province. In 1987 a new

State-owned bank was established in the South, offering competitively high interest rates and attracted deposits faster than the bank could expand its operations to handle them.

78. *SWB*, FE/7949/B/4, 13 May 1985.
79. *SWB*, FE/W1372/A/38-39, 15 January 1986.
80. Tran Thanh Phuong, *Nhung Trang Ve An Giang*, pp. 104, 121. According to this source the ratio fell from 1.3 in 1975 to 0.6 in 1980.
81. Tan Ba, which complained of fertiliser shortages 'sometimes', was in fact by far the heaviest user of chemical fertilisers; possibly it was compensating by hoarding. Quyet Thang complained of delivery delays rather than shortages (though the consequences for production can be the same).
82. Based on information from provincial authorities and emigrant sources Lam Thanh Liem ('Nouvelles reformes et crise persistante de l'économie rurale dans le delta du Mekong de 1981 à 1985', *Annales de Géographie*, no. 524, July-August 1985) estimates effective tax-rates ranging from 10 per cent of the harvest on category 7 land (the worst) to 28 per cent on category 1 land (the best), (p. 398). In addition, he says there was a supplementary tax to reduce inequality between private and cooperative cultivators ranging from nil on landholdings of less than 0.5 ha to 40 per cent of the harvest on holdings of 3–5 ha. The emigrant sources on yields (no size of sample given) are also used to suggest that official statistics on output after 1983 are a gross overestimation.
     In fact land should be assessed for tax according to average yields over a three-year period (see Ministry of Finance, *Nhung Van De Chu Yeu Trong Phap Lenh Thue Nong Nghiep*, (Hanoi: Su That, 1985) p. 35). It is Vietnamese practice to allow remissions in cases of major crop failure, so it is not clear why Liem's tax-rates are so high, unless part of a policy, now abandoned, of squeezing private agriculture.
83. I was told that this was due to bomb craters which, when filled in, created a soft bottom to canals and made construction of irrigation works difficult.
84. Vo Van Kiet, *Thuc Hien Dong Bo 3 Cuoc Cach Mang o Nong Thon*, Nha Xuat Ban Thanh Pho Ho Chi Minh (1985) pp. 103–4, 106.
85. This is extensively discussed in relation to Vietnam in Nyland, op. cit. See also Phan Le Phuong, 'Several Thoughts Concerning the Application of Market Relations in Planning', *So Tay Giang Vien*, No. 6, November 1977, translated in JPRS 70675, *Translations on Vietnam* no. 2013, p. 54; Trinh Xuan Tien (Vice-Minister of Food) 'The Present Management of the Grain Market', *Tap Chi Cong San*, no. 11, November 1979, translated in JPRS 74929, *Vietnam Report* no. 2164, p. 62.
86. In Le Duan and Pham Van Dong, *Towards Large-Scale Socialist Agricultural Production* (Hanoi: FLPH, 1975, pp. 32–33).

Chapter Five   Household and Collective in Vietnamese Agriculture

1. General Statistical Office, *Tinh Hinh Phat Trien Kinh Te va Van Hoa Mien Bac Xa Hoi Chu Nghia Viet Nam 1960–1975* (Economic and Cultural Development in Socialist North Vietnam 1960–1975), Hanoi,

1978, p. 132; English translation in Adam Fforde and Suzanne Paine, *The Limits of National Liberation* (London: Croom Helm, 1987).

2. See, for example, the article by Nguyen Huu Dong, 'Agriculture Collective, Agriculture Familiale, Économie Socialiste: Quelques Hypothèses', *Vietnam*, No. 1, December 1980, pp. 22–3.

3. Indeed the response of the Government of North Vietnam was to make such contracting in land illegal. See Kim Ngoc, 'Determined to Correct the Shortcomings and Steadily Advance the Cooperativisation Movement and Agricultural Production in Vinh Phu Province', *Hoc Tap*, no. 6, June 1969, translated in JPRS, *Translations on North Vietnam*, no. 583, and Alec Gordon, 'North Vietnam's Collectivisation Campaigns', *Journal of Contemporary Asia*, vol. 11 (1981) no. 1.

4. A. Watson, 'Agriculture Looks for "Shoes that Fit": the Production Responsibility System and its Implications', in N. Maxwell and B. McFarlane (eds) *China's Changed Road to Development* (Oxford: Pergamon Press, 1984).

5. US Department of Agriculture estimates for DRV net imports of rice from China between 1969 and 1974 are as follows (in 000 tonnes): 1969, 527; 1970, 465; 1971, 433; 1972, 565; 1973, 490; 1974, 564 (A. Siamwalla and S. Haykin, *The World Rice Market: Structure, Conduct and Performance*, International Food Policy Research Institute, Research Report no. 39, June 1983, p. 66. These estimates coincide with another estimate for the early 1970s of about 0.5 million tonnes per annum by Adam Fforde, *Problems of Agricultural Development in North Vietnam*, PhD thesis, University of Cambridge, 1982, pp. 49–50.

6. Chinese commodity aid was terminated as early as 1975. In spite of this, the leadership did expect substantial quantities of such aid in the short-term and the rather ambitious investment targets of the Second Five-Year Plan (1976–80) can be explained by the over-optimistic expectations on this score.

7. For a discussion of the new management system see 'The Management of Cooperatives', *Vietnamese Studies* (special issue on Agricultural Problems), no. 51, n.d., and A. Fforde, op. cit.

8. In fact only three kinds of task are normally contracted under the Government's preferred system. These are transplanting, cultivation and harvesting. Soil preparation, seed selection and breeding, fertilisation, irrigation and pesticide control should be left to the collective (except possibly where animals are used in the first of these). The contracted tasks are usually carried out by women, who, as Christine White has pointed out, are thereby relegated to the more 'backward' areas of the economy while men predominate in the technically more advanced occupations ('Reforming Relations of Production: Family and Cooperative in Vietnamese Agricultural Policy', mimeo, Institute of Development Studies, University of Sussex).

9. If Hinton is right, this constitutes a major difference with the Chinese experience since the Vietnamese continue to regard mechanisation and industrialisation of agriculture as of key importance. Hinton, however, cites Chinese officials as saying that land and its distribution are the key to development, and that class exploitation cannot exist except as a

result of usury, speculation or land rent. He also reports cases where demechanisation has taken place (William Hinton, 'More on China's New Family Contract System', *Monthly Review*, April 1984, p. 44; see also his 'A Trip to Fengyang County', *Monthly Review*, November 1983, pp. 18, 24). Peter Nolan, on the other hand, reports that over most of the country, 'large' means of production (tractors, trucks, large sprayers, irrigation facilities, processing apparatus) have tended (though not exclusively) to be retained by the collective under the new system ('From Collective Farms to Cooperatives', *China Now* (1984) no. 108, Spring, p. 17) and this would also seem to apply to Hinton's own description of Fengyang County.

10.   Calculated from *So Lieu Thong Ke 1979* (Hanoi: General Statistical Office, 1980) pp. 58–59.

11.   Fforde, op. cit., p. 130.

12.   Ibid., p. 132. This presumably refers to the existence of more 'backward' forms of income distribution such as payment of rent for land contributed to the cooperative or possibly the existence of abuses of power by managers and cadres in order to enhance their own incomes, rather than excessive egalitarianism which was later to become a main point of criticism.

13.   Ibid., p. 134.

14.   Le Thu Y, 'Improve Planning in Agricultural Cooperatives' (*Nghien Cuu Kinh Te*, (1975) no. 87, September-October, pp. 41–53), English translation in *Translations on Vietnam*, no. 1759, JPRS 66638.

15.   Ibid., p. 27.

16.   Hoang Anh ('Pricing Activities in the New Situation', *Tap Chi Cong San*, (1978) no. 6, June, translated in *Translations on Vietnam*, no. 2057, JPRS 71773, p. 56) says that the material costs and consumption of labour power in producing a quintal of paddy had increased over an unspecified period. High and rising labour costs per unit of output may well have come from the labour accumulation projects themselves: large irrigation schemes not only give lower returns as poorer land is brought into their scope, but require more labour for both construction and maintenance, unless mechanisation is introduced. According to Le Thanh Khoi (*Socialisme et Developpement au Vietnam* (Paris: Presses Universitaires de France, 1978) pp. 129–30), it took 120–140 hours to produce 100 kg of rice in North Vietnam. This compared with 44.4 hours in Japan and 1.3 in the USA.

17.   Le Thu Y, op. cit., p. 27.

18.   21 June 1978; translated in *Translations on Vietnam*, no. 2057, JPRS 71654, p. 59.

19.   Fforde, op. cit., p. 189.

20.   Amit Bhaduri, *Agricultural Cooperatives in North Vietnam* Rural Employment Policy Research Programme, Working paper WEP 10/WP/6 (Geneva: ILO, March 1976) p. 29. For case studies from other socialist countries see, for example, C. Humphrey, *Karl Marx Collective* (Cambridge and Paris: Cambridge University Press and Éditions de la Maison des Sciences de l'Homme, 1983), pp. 261–2; Peter Nolan, 'De-Collectivi-

sation of Agriculture in China 1979–82: A Long-Term Perspective', *Economic and Political Weekly,* 6 August 1983.

21.   V. I. Lenin, 'The Agrarian Question and the Critics of Marx' [1901], *Collected Works,* vol. 5 (Moscow: Progress Publishers, 1973), pp. 161–2.

22.   The confusion over what 'large-scale' means in the agricultural context is quite common. M. Ellman (*Socialist Planning* (Cambridge University Press, 1979), p. 88), for example, cites uncritically the work of Michael Lipton and others, who purport to show the superiority of small-*sized* farms over larger-sized ones, when in fact the superiority exists only where traditional, labour-intensive methods are used. Where mechanisation is able to do away with the labour-supervision constraint, this inverse relationship between productivity and size disappears (see Abhijit Sen, 'Market Failure and Control of Labour Power: Towards an Explanation of "Structure" and Change in Indian Agriculture', Parts I and II, *Cambridge Journal of Economics,* vol. 5, (1981) nos. 3 & 4. Lenin also emphasised that 'large scale' referred to the capital-intensity and not to the size of the farm (see his 'The Agrarian Question . . .', op. cit., and 'New Data on the Laws Governing the Development of Capitalism in Agriculture', [1915], *Collected Works,* vol. 22 (Moscow: Progress Publishers, 1964).

23.   Le Duan, General Secretary of the Communist Party of Vietnam, speaking at an agricultural conference in 1974, based his argument for proceeding with collectivisation in the absence of industrialisation on the assertion that only through collectivisation would it be possible to achieve large-scale water conservancy and soil improvement. He stated that the 'national democratic revolution', rather than the development of large-scale industry, had created the pre-conditions for socialist transformation, Le Duan and Pham Van Dong, *Towards Large-Scale Socialist Agricultural Production* (Hanoi: FLPH 1975), p. 32.

24.   Le Thu Y, op. cit., p. 19.

25.   'De-collectivisation . . .', op. cit.

26.   The Vietnamese Minister of Agriculture announced that as a result of the decisions of the 6th CPV Central Committee Plenum introducing economic reforms in 1979, it would be possible in poor years to have a zero accumulation fund. *Nhan Dan,* 14 November 1979 (translated in *Vietnam Report,* no. 2161, JPRS 74810, p. 50).

27.   These ideas were originally associated with Soviet writers like Preobrazhensky and Feldman who argued that the rate of growth depended entirely on the growth in the investment goods sector (because the rate of growth of consumer goods production depended upon the rate of increase of means of production in the consumer goods sector). An influential Western writer in this school is Maurice Dobb (*An Essay on Economic Growth and Planning,* London: Routledge & Kegan Paul, 1960).

28.   Michal Kalecki, *Selected Essays on the Economic Growth of the Socialist and Mixed Economy* (Cambridge University Press, 1972); Adolf Lowe, 'Structural Analysis of Real Capital Formation' in Universities-National Bureau Committee of Economic Research, *Capital Formation and*

Economic Growth: A Conference, National Bureau of Economic Research, Princeton University Press, 1955.

29. For a discussion of this see D. L. Clark, 'Planning and the Real Origins of Input-Output Analysis', *Journal of Contemporary Asia*, vol. 14 (1984) no. 4.

30. I. Norlund, 'The Role of Industry in Vietnam's Development Strategy', *Journal of Contemporary Asia*, vol. 14 (1984) no. 1, pp. 95–6, 103–4.

31. Hoang Duc Nghi, 'Making Rational and Economic Use of Material Resources in the National Economy', *Tap Chi Hoat Dong Khoa Hoc*, no. 7, July 1982, translated in JPRS 82098, *Vietnam Report* no. 2405.

32. Nancy Gonzalez, 'The Organisation of Work in China's Communes', *Science*, vol. 217 (1982) no. 4563, 3 September, p. 903.

33. *Asia Yearbook 1982*, (Hong Kong: Far Eastern Economic Review, 1982) p. 262.

34. See *Nhan Dan*, 19 June 1978, (translated in *Translations on Vietnam*, no. 2052, p. 12) on the diversion of scarce state goods to the free market.

35. 'De-collectivisation . . .', op. cit.

36. *Far Eastern Economic Review*, 28 April 1988.

37. See Christine White, 'Agricultural Planning, Pricing Policy and Co-operatives in Vietnam', *World Development*, vol. 13 (1985) no. 1, pp. 105–106. Hoang Anh (op. cit., pp. 56–7) reports that procurement prices of agricultural products were raised after 1973 while prices of means of production and consumer goods bought by farmers fell.

38. In any case, Le Thu Y (op. cit., p. 22) says that unofficial figures for 1973 show 25–30 per cent of cooperatives suffering net losses.

39. Official procurement prices for some principal agricultural products were increased by the following percentages in October 1981: paddy, 381–483 (depending on local conditions); maize, 323–392; sweet potato, 323–392; cassava, 260–433. Input prices, supplied by the State under the two-way contract system rose in September 1981 by the following percentages: (north and central Vietnam only): petroleum, 1207; diesel oil, 1555; urea, 1346; electricity, 0. It should be noted that the first three items here are largely imported and the increases were needed to offset the effects of devaluation of the dong. Other input prices rose within the range 400–600 per cent. See International Monetary Fund, 'Socialist Republic of Vietnam – Recent Economic Developments', SM/82/96, 18 May 1982, pp. 36–7.

40. Nolan, 'De-collectivisation . . .', op. cit.

41. D. Ghai, A. Rahman Khan, E. Lee, S. Radwen, *Agrarian Systems and Rural Development* (London: Macmillan, 1979), p. 266.

42. Sen, op. cit.

43. This point can be compared with Marx's discussion of the control over the labour process exercised by workers in the manufactories of early industrialisation: 'Since handicraft skill is the foundation of manufacture, and since the mechanism of manufacture as a whole possesses no framework, apart from the labourers themselves, capital is constantly compelled to wrestle with the insubordination of the workmen'. K. Marx, *Capital*, vol.1, (Moscow: Progress, n.d.) p.346. Also: 'throughout the whole manufacturing period there runs the complaint of want of discipline among the workmen' (p.347).

Systems of supervision and remuneration reflected this. Where workers were concentrated under a single roof, it was possible to maintain the pace and quality of work by close supervision. In cases where workers were spatially dispersed and supervision difficult, incentives to work hard and well were incorporated into the remuneration system via piece-rates or other productivity-linked wage setting.

44. In the case of the Soviet collective studied by Caroline Humphrey, factors in the technological environment such as an unreliable electricity supply and bottlenecks caused by unmechanised parts of the production process contributed to the failure of livestock mechanisation (op. cit., pp. 178–179). Nguyen Huu Dong has documented cases of successful and unsuccessful attempts to mechanise farming in Vietnam (op. cit., pp. 20–1). S. Ishikawa, based on a study of a number of Asian countries, including China, has concluded that the appropriate technology will depend upon (i) endowment of capital, labour and resources; (ii) technological capability; (iii) managerial capability; (iv) structure of demand for products; (v) degree of development of the market; (vi) determinants in foreign countries with which the agricultural economy is related; (*Essays on Technology, Employment and Institutions in Development: Comparative Asian Experience* (Tokyo: Kikokuniya, 1981) especially p. 351.

45. Op. cit., p. 903. Gonzalez visited the Yangzi delta, industrially advanced areas around Shenyang in Liaoning province as well as less developed areas of Anhui and Guangdong.

46. Although the terms 'private sector' and 'private plot' are most often used in Western literature on this topic, their use does rather prejudice the issue as they have very definite connotations of 'private property'. I prefer to use the term 'household', 'family' or 'individual' in preference, except where I am referring to arguments which explicitly place household production within the sphere of private property.

47. This view is based loosely on Marx's writings in the *Critique of the Gotha Programme*.

48. Data on the USSR can be found in Karl-Eugen Wadekin, *The Private Sector in Soviet Agriculture* (Berkeley: University of California Press, 1973). However, this also shows that the share of the private sector in agricultural output declined between 1953 and 1969 and the index for private production had stagnated since 1958 (pp. 52–66).

49. According to Bhaduri (op. cit.) private land in North Vietnam was almost three times as productive as cooperative sector land. *Nhan Dan* of 21 June 1978 (op. cit) points to one case where the yield on cooperative land was only 60–70 per cent of that on family plots. It is not stated whether these figures refer to the same crops on both types of land. In 1979 the then Minister for Agriculture, Duong Hong Dat, stated in an interview for *Tap Chi Hoat Dong Khoa Hoc* (Scientific Review) (no. 9, September 1979) that a survey of family plots had revealed that one hectare of land 'in any location' normally yielded 7–8 tonnes of 5th month or winter-spring rice and 4–5 tonnes of 10th month rice. For the former crop, the national average in 1979 was 1.9 tonnes (a fall from 2.7 in 1976) (Translated in JPRS 74779, *Vietnam Report*, no. 2159, pp. 35–7). Le Duc Tho claimed, in a 1982 report, that 5 per cent plots 'got

proper care and yielded twice more than the collective'; 'Improve Agricultural Management', *Southeast Asia Chronicle*, no. 93, April 1984, p. 7.

50. Le Thu Y, op. cit. Christine White provides an excellent survey of the debate surrounding this issue in 'Debates on Vietnamese Development Policy', Institute of Development Studies, *Discussion Paper*, no. 171, University of Sussex, March 1982.

51. A factor which has been well documented by Caroline Humphrey in the case of Siberian collective farms of the USSR (op. cit., pp. 433–5). For the Vietnamese case, see Fforde, op. cit., p. 80; Le Thu Y, op. cit., p. 36; also *Vietnamese Studies*, no. 51, p. 168.

52. Nguyen Xuan Lai, 'The Family Economy of Co-operative Farmers', *Vietnamese Studies*, no. 13 (n.d.), pp. 107–28.

53. Nguyen Huu Dong, op. cit., pp. 22–3. The advocacy of a 12-hour day seems to me to be a rather extreme position to take, but as we have seen above, the actual situation is not one in which such high quantities of labour are extracted.

54. Christine White 'Socialist Transformation of Agriculture and Gender Relations: The Vietnamese Case', *IDS Bulletin*, vol. 13, (1982) no. 4, September, p. 48.

55. It was precisely the existence of an expanding manufacturing-based economy which showed Marx the inadequacy of the Ricardo/Malthus idea of 'subsistence' as minimum physical requirements for survival (corn) and caused him to introduce the concept of *socially necessary* means of subsistence. As the economy becomes increasingly sophisticated, so the rural population's need for cash income to purchase manufactured consumer goods rises, but this in itself does not denote the existence of economic surpluses in peasant households.

56. It is a paradox of the distribution system adopted in Vietnamese cooperatives that it is necessary labour and not the surplus which is the residual. Labour remuneration is determined after norms for tax, quota sales and accumulation funds have been met. Surpluses may, therefore, have been extracted at the cost of reducing labour remuneration below subsistence level, providing further incentive to transfer labour into household production. The result is that efforts to extract any surplus are likely to become increasingly difficult.

57. Here again the contrast with the Chinese 'production responsibility system' is important. Clearly if peasants are able to accumulate modern means of production and dispose of them freely, then an alternative economic power to that of the collective will arise. Such is still the case for much of the Mekong delta area of southern Vietnam, but the Vietnamese leadership do not envisage extending this to the already collectivised areas of northern and central Vietnam. *Nhan Dan,* on 22 October 1979 argued that 'Petty individual production or petty trade can only develop into capitalism through a process of accumulation of capital and its use in capitalist enterprises, creating private ownership or large-scale means of production. The proletarian state and socialist economy do not allow this to happen' (translated by Christine White in 'Reforming Relations of Production . . .', op. cit., p. 17).

58. *Far Eastern Economic Review*, 28 April 1988, p. 76.
59. Exceptions to this no doubt exist, but they are frowned upon, see Le Duc Tho, op. cit., p. 11).
60. Cited in Trinh Xuan Tien, 'The Present State of the Grain Market', *Tap Chi Cong San*, no. 11, November 1979, JPRS 74929, *Vietnam Report*, no. 2164, p. 63.
61. 'New Data on the Laws Governing the Development of Capitalism in Agriculture', op. cit., p. 59.
62. This is confirmed by the Soviet writer Lukinov: 'The attempts to artificially reduce the sales of products at higher prices on the markets (after the fulfilment of the procurement plans) checks the growth of Kholkhoz revenues and is often accompanied by a revival of speculation.' (Cited in Wadekin, op. cit., p. 178) While the statement refers to market sales by collective farms rather than individuals, it nevertheless gives an insight into the practical results of administrative methods ('*dirigisme*' or 'commandism') as a method of controlling market activities. Wadekin also reported that restriction of private plots caused people to move into cities or to take up alternative, illegal occupations (p. 206).

Chapter Six   The Vietnamese Industrialisation Debate

1. In April 1976 it was reported that 1.6m tonnes of goods had been transported from North to South since April 1975, including rice, sugar, fuel, industrial raw materials and equipment, fertiliser, medicine, 32m metres of cloth, 1700 tonnes of seeds and thousands of livestock. In return the South had exported 80 000 tonnes to the North. BBC *Summary of World Broadcasts*, FE/W875/A/27, 28 April 1976.
2. The 1931 paddy price was only 46 per cent of its 1924–8 average. P. Bernard, *Le Problème économique indochinois* (Paris: Nouvelles Éditions Latines, 1934) p. 99.
3. Le Chau, *Le Vietnam socialiste: une économie de transition* (Paris: Maspero, 1966) p. 225.
4. Andrew Vickerman, 'A Note on the Role of Industry in Vietnam's Development Strategy', *Journal of Contemporary Asia*, vol. 15 (1985) no. 2, p. 224.
5. Calculated from data in Bernard, op. cit., pp. 14, 26–7.
6. Doan Trong Truyen and Pham Thanh Vinh, *L'Edification d'une Économie nationale indépendante au Vietnam (1945–65)* (Hanoi: Éditions en langues étrangères, 1966) p. 126 (my translation).
7. See, for example, S. Pollard, *Peaceful Conquest: the Industrialisation of Europe 1760–1970* (Oxford University Press, 1981); UN Economic Commission for Europe, *Economic Survey of Europe in 1957*, Geneva, 1958; N. Spulber, *The Economies of Communist Eastern Europe* (New York: Technology Press and John Wiley, Chapman & Hall, 1957). China, Cuba, North Korea and Vietnam have all also followed this path at some stage.
8. Maurice Dobb, *Papers on Capitalism, Development and Planning* (London: Routledge & Kegan Paul, 1967).

Notes to Chapter 6

9. L. G. Stolleru, 'An Optimal Policy for Economic Growth', *Econometrica*, vol. 33, (1965) no. 2, April.

10. Kalecki's basic growth model is set out in the equation $r = {}^1/_{Y} \cdot {}^1/_m - a + u$ where 'r' is the rate of growth; '${}^1/_Y$' is the share of investment in national income; '${}^1/_m$' is the reciprocal of the capital–output ratio (i.e., it represents the productive effect of investment); 'a' is the depreciation rate of the existing capital stock and 'u' refers to 'improvements in the utilisation of equipment which do not require significant capital outlays, improvements in organisation of labour, more economical use of raw materials, elimination of faulty products etc. As a result of such efforts the national income increases at the beginning of the next year by an amount $uY - u$ being the coefficient which represents the effect of such improvements' See Michal Kalecki, *Selected Essays on the Economic Growth of the Socialist and Mixed Economy* (Cambridge University Press, 1972) p. 11.

11. General Statistical Office, *Tinh Hinh Phat Trien Kinh Te va Van Hoa Mien Bac Xa Hoi Chu Nghia Viet Nam 1960–1975,* Hanoi, 1978, p. 151.

12. Measured in million passenger kilometres. Ibid., p. 168.

13. A. Siamwalla and S. Haykin, 'The World Rice Market: Structure, Conduct and Performance', International Food Policy Research Institute, June 1983, p. 66; Adam Fforde and Suzanne H. Paine (*The Limits of National Liberation* (London: Croom Helm, 1987) p. 69) give Soviet food exports to Vietnam.

14. W. Kaye 'A Bowl of Rice Divided: The Economy of North Vietnam' in P. J. Honey (ed.) *North Vietnam Today* (New York: Praeger, 1962) p. 115.

15. G. Nguyen Tien Hung, *Economic Development of Socialist Vietnam, 1955–80* (New York: Praeger 1977) p. 185.

16. Nigel Thrift and Dean Forbes, *The Price of War: Urbanization in Vietnam 1954–1985* (London: Allen & Unwin, 1986) p. 72.

17. Le Chau, op. cit., p. 246.

18. Nguyen Tien Hung, op. cit., p. 89.

19. Le Chau, op. cit., p. 205.

20. Vo Nhan Tri, *Croissance économique de la République democratique du Vietnam (1945–1965)* (Hanoi: Éditions en langues étrangères, 1967) pp. 557–8.

21. *Tinh Hinh Kinh Te Mien Nam 1955–1975 (THKTMN)*, Ho Chi Minh City: Institute of Social Sciences, 1979, p. 47.

22. Vickerman, op. cit., p. 229; General Statistical Office, *Tinh Hinh Phat Trien ...*, p. 152.

23. *THKTMN*, p. 47.

24. The Three Year Plan (1958–60) stipulated that external aid should finance investment at an average of 305 million dong per annum (Nguyen Tien Hung, op. cit., p. 89). On the basis of these figures, those on the producer goods content of actual aid in the three years and value of domestically produced capital goods (as measured by output value of Group A – ibid., p. 140), it is possible to estimate that roughly 35–40 per cent of the annual supply of producer goods derived from foreign aid in this period.

25. N. Bukharin 'Notes of an Economist at the Beginning of a New Economic Year', in N. Spulber (ed.), *Foundations of Soviet Strategy for Economic Growth* (Bloomington: University of Indiana Press, 1964) p. 262.

26. Ibid., p. 263.

27. Ibid.

28. See R. Kalain, 'Mao Tse Tung's "Bukharinist" Phase', *Journal of Contemporary Asia,* vol. 14, (1984) no. 2. Some of the more recent debates in China in the late 1970s were published in Xu Dixin et al., *China's Search for Economic Growth* (Beijing: New World Press, 1982).

29. J. Kornai, *Growth, Shortage and Efficiency* (Oxford: Basil Blackwell, 1982).

30. See also Bruce McFarlane, 'Political Economy of Class Struggle and Economic Growth in China, 1950–1982' (*World Development,* vol. 11 (1983) no. 8, and the same author's 'Political Crisis and East European Economic Reforms' (in Paul G. Lewis (ed.), *Eastern Europe: Political Crisis and Legitimation,* (London and Sydney: Croom Helm, 1984) for discussion of a political cycle in socialist countries.

31. This important passage is left out of Spulber's translation. See Richard B. Day (ed.), *Selected Writings on the State and the Transition to Socialism* (New York: M. E. Sharpe, 1982) and also *Economy and Society,* vol. 8 (1979) no. 4, p. 478.

32. See Preobrazhensky's essay 'On Economic Equilibrium in the USSR', in Donald A. Filtzer (ed.), *The Crisis of Soviet Industrialization* (London and New York: Macmillan and M. E. Sharpe, 1980).

33. Adolph Lowe, among others, pointed out that within the capital goods sector, there is a further vitally important proportional relationship, that between Department Ia, or capital goods producing capital goods (machines to produce machines), and Department Ib, or machines to produce consumer goods (i.e. the balance between the iron and steel, or machine tools industries and industries producing looms, canning apparatus, tractors, etc.). See his 'A Structural Approach to Capital Formation', in Universities-National Bureau of Economic Research, *Capital Formation and Economic Growth: A Conference* (Princeton University Press, 1955).

34. JPRS, *Vietnam Report* no. 2162, p. 65.

35. Danh Son, 'Raw Materials in the Effort to Build and Perfect the Production Structure in Our Country', *Nghien Cuu Kinh Te,* December 1981, translated in JPRS 80671, *Vietnam Report* no. 2361, p. 29.

36. Problems were also caused in this sector by changes in the planned product mix from year to year and the fact that firms were not receiving plans until half the year was gone. Ho Ngoc Minh 'Several Matters Regarding Labour Management Within the Machine Enterprises of Ho Chi Minh City', *Nghien Cuu Kinh Te,* December 1979, translated in JPRS 75471, *Vietnam Report* no. 2181, pp. 66–70.

37. JPRS 75637, *Vietnam Report* no. 2187, pp. 50–1.

38. Danh Son, op. cit., p. 29.

39. JPRS 75637, *Vietnam Report* no. 2187, p. 64.

40. JPRS 75401, *Vietnam Report* no. 2179, p. 30.

41.   JPRS 75456, *Vietnam Report* no. 2180. pp. 31–4.
42.   Danh Son, op. cit., p. 29.
43.   JPRS 75858, *Vietnam Report* no. 2193, pp. 38–9.
44.   JPRS 75666, *Vietnam Report* no. 2188, pp. 46–7.
45.   General Statistical Office, *So Lieu Thong Ke 1930–1984*, (Hanoi, 1985) p. 82. The agricultural area did not decline, but yields per hectare did (see ibid., pp. 85, 87).
46.   Ho Ngoc Minh, op. cit., p. 66.
47.   The coal industry, for example, was severely affected and ethnic Chinese also formed a high proportion of workers in major northern industrial centres like Nam Dinh and Haiphong.
48.   Nguyen Huu Dong, 'Quelques Caractéristiques de l'Industrialisation au Vietnam', mimeo, Symposium on 'Tradition und Wandel in Vietnam', University of Hamburg, October 1978, p. 24. Estimates of Chinese food aid to the DRV were given in Chapter 5 in the present book. The total amount of Chinese aid to Vietnam is not known, but among Chinese-assisted projects completed or underway during 1976 were: an antibiotic factory at Viet Tri, extension and improvement to Viet Tri chemical works, restoration and expansion of Thai Nguyen iron and steel works, the central Post Office in Hanoi, Bim Son cement works, a glassware factory in Hai Hung province, Vinh Phu textile complex, Ninh Binh thermal power station (100 MW) and a printing factory. (See *SWB*, FE/W883/A/26, 23 June 1976; FE/W875/A/26, 28 April 1976; FE/W900/A/36, 20 October 1976; FE/W902/A/34, 3 November 1976; FE/W903/A/36, 10 November 1976; FE/W909/A/35, 22 December 1976; FE/W911/A/35, 12 January 1977; FE/W912/A/37, 19 January 1977.)
49.   The vital chemical fertiliser industry, for example, due to the destruction of the apatite ore mine at Lao Cai (very close to the Chinese border). At Lang Son a large anise oil factory, built with French assistance, was completely destroyed in February 1979.
50.   This expectation was based on commitments given by Henry Kissinger at the peace talks in Paris to provide $US3.2bn in reconstruction assistance to Vietnam after the war. These commitments were rejected by Congress in May 1976 after ten minutes' debate.
51.   Plans were announced for the preparatory stages of construction of an oil refinery, a synthetic fibre factory and expansion of the oil-based chemical industry, but it is not known if any of these highly capital-intensive schemes were actually started (Communist Party of Viet Nam, *4th National Congress Documents* (Hanoi: FLPH 1977) p. 72). In fact no significant oil discoveries were made until 1984 (*SWB*, FE/W1290/A/21, 6 June 1984).
52.   Truong Chinh, 'CPV Congress Political Report', *SWB*, FE/8447/C1/18–20, 24, 20 December 1986.
53.   Le Duan, 'Get a good hold of the laws and renovate economic management', *Viet Nam Social Sciences*, no. 2, 1984, pp. 9–10.
54.   *SWB*, FE/8453/B/6, 31 December 1986.
55.   In the machinery industry, small industry and handicrafts produced 27.1 per cent of output value in 1975 and 53.9 per cent in 1983; in chemicals

the shift was from 17.8 per cent in 1975 to 30.3 per cent in 1983. *So Lieu Thong Ke 1930–84*, pp. 49, 50.

56. *So Lieu Thong Ke 1930–1984*, pp. 35, 74.
57. National Assembly resolution on the 1986 economic plan, *SWB*, FE/8152/C1/1, 9 January 1986.
58. Truong Chinh, op. cit., pp. 5, 22.
59. *Far Eastern Economic Review*, 24 May 1984, pp. 80–1.
60. *SWB*, FE/W1303/A/18, 5 September 1984.
61. *SWB*, FE/W1369/A/33, December 1985.
62. *SWB*, FE/W1343/A/28, 19 June 1985.
63. For details, see Chapter 7.
64. Nguyen Van Linh, *Thanh Pho Ho Chi Minh 10 Nam* (Hanoi: Su That, 1985) pp. 105–6.
65. *Cuu Long Thanh Tuu 10 Nam* (Ho Chi Minh City: Nha Xuat Ban Cuu Long, 1985) pp. 78, 80.
66. *So Lieu Thong Ke 1930–1984*, pp. 42, 69.
67. Le Duan, op. cit., pp. 10–11.
68. The priorities for the 1981–5 plan were usually listed as: agriculture, consumer goods industry, oil and energy, exports and communications. See, for example, *Far Eastern Economic Review*, 29 January 1982, p. 49. During the 1986–1990 period, agriculture, consumer goods and exports are the three main areas, with particular emphasis on consolidating and improving per capita availability of food.
69. Uy Ban Khoa Hoc Xa Hoi Viet Nam, *35 Nam Kinh Te Viet Nam 1945–1980*, (Hanoi: Nha Xuat Ban Khoa Hoc Xa Hoi, 1980) p. 97.
70. Christine Pelzer White, 'Debates in Vietnamese Development Policy', *IDS Discussion Paper*, University of Sussex, Brighton, 1982, p. 10.
71. *So Lieu Thong Ke 1930–1984*, p. 44; *SWB*, FE/W1421/A/29, 31 December 1986.
72. Thomas G. Rawski, *China's Transition to Industrialism*, (Ann Arbor: University of Michigan Press, 1980) pp. 22–4.
73. However, the effects of military mobilisation are probably less of a drag on economic growth than is commonly supposed in the West. According to an IMF report, cited in the *Far Eastern Economic Review* (15 November 1984, p. 130), the cost of maintaining the army is of relatively minor importance in relation to other problems (consumption subsidies, for example). The biggest drain on resources caused by the army is said to be the absorption of too many technicians and too much scarce transportation. Most equipment comes from Soviet aid and in the 1980s Vietnam has not been one of the major Third World arms importers, nor even one of the the Soviet Union's main customers (*SIPRI Yearbook*, Stockholm, 1987, pp. 187, 201). The army is used in economic development projects (e.g. in clearing and constructing new economic zones, preparatory to opening them for settlement) maintains its own state farms, particularly in the border zones, and is engaged in building roads, housing, irrigation schemes and growing industrial crops. See *SWB*, FE/W1421/A/30, 31 December 1986.
74. *SWB*, FE/8139/B/5, 20 December 1985.

75.   Ibid., p. B/8.
76.   See, for example, editorial of *Tap Chi Cong San,* no. 10, October 1979, translated in JPRS 74807, *Vietnam Report* no. 2160, p. 7.
77.   Le Van Hoan 'Thoughts Based on the Reality of Trieu Hai', *Tap Chi Cong San,* no. 12, December 1981, translated in JPRS 80226, *Vietnam Report* no. 2349, p. 46.
78.   JPRS 75471, *Vietnam Report* no. 2181, p. 55.
79.   *SWB,* FE/8154/B/3, 11 January 1986.
80.   Truong Chinh, op. cit., p. 23.
81.   Ibid.
82.   Ibid., p. 20.
83.   Ibid., p. 24.
84.   *Financial Times,* 11 May 1987.
85.   There are no official figures. One estimate of urban unemployment given to the *Far Eastern Economic Review* (23 July 1987, p. 29) by an unnamed Vietnamese economist was one million. This would be about 13 per cent of the urban population of working age.
86.   'Vo Van Kiet's Economic Report', *SWB,* FE/8449/C1/12, 23 December 1986.
87.   Truong Chinh, op. cit., p. 22.
88.   Nguyen Duc Thuan, president of the Vietnam Confederation of Trade Unions, reported in *Nhan Dan,* 6 April 1982.
89.   JPRS 75945, *Vietnam Report* no. 2197, p. 20.
90.   JPRS 75456, *Vietnam Report* no. 2180, p. 37.
91.   JPRS 80977, *Vietnam Report* no. 2369, p. 36.
92.   Speech by Pham Ngoc Bich, director of the Nam Dinh Textile Combine, to 5th Party Congress, JPRS 81347, *Vietnam Report* no. 2381, p. 64.
93.   JPRS 81888, *Vietnam Report* no. 2397, p. 28.
94.   IMF, 'Viet Nam – Staff Report for the 1983 Article IV Consultation', 13 June 1983, p. 4.
95.   *Far Eastern Economic Review,* 10 April 1986. Max Spoor ('Finance in a Socialist Transition: the case of the Democratic Republic of Vietnam 1955–64' *Journal of Contemporary Asia,* vol. 17 (1987) no. 3, p. 349) discusses similar measures taken in 1959 with similar results.
96.   Cf. Liu Guoguang, 'Aspects and Problems of Price Reform in China', mimeo, Centre for Asian Studies, University of Adelaide, 1986.
97.   See M. Beresford, 'Vietnam: Northernizing the South or Southernizing the North?, *Contemporary Southeast Asia,* vol. 8, (1987) no. 3, p. 266.
98.   *SWB,* FE/8139/B/5, 20 December 1985.

Chapter Seven   Socialist Commodity Production

1.   See O. Kyn 'The Role of Prices in a Socialist Economy', in M. C. Kaser (ed.), *Economic Development for Eastern Europe,* (London and New York: Macmillan and St. Martins Press, 1968) for a summary of the East European debate and S. Reglar, 'The Law of Value Debate – A Tribute to the Late Sun Yefang' in Bill Brugger (ed.), *Marxism in Flux 1978–1984* (London and Sydney: Croom Helm, 1985) for the Chinese debate.
2.   Because of the conflicting signals given under the former pricing system,

this had already taken place in a *de facto* way in Vietnam, even before the reforms. See Christine White, 'Agricultural Planning, Pricing Policy and Co-operatives in Vietnam', *World Development,* vol. 13 (1985) no. 1.

3. Ibid., p. 98.
4. In 1955 the State share of wholesale trade was 28 per cent; in 1957 it had grown to 53 per cent and by 1960 it was 94 per cent according to Vo Nhan Tri (*Croissance économique de la République démocratique du Vietnam* (Hanoi: FLPH, 1966) pp. 239, 333).
5. Ibid., p. 241.
6. However, there is a problem of valuation of agricultural production. As Christine White has pointed out (op. cit., p. 104), official prices for paddy appear to have been based on costs of production in the most advanced cooperatives and the method of valuing labour is not known. I tried to find out how agricultural labour is valued during my visit to Vietnam in 1985, but was told only that it was measured in terms of paddy which would appear to involve some circularity.
7. General Statistical Office, *Tinh Hinh Phat Trien Kinh Te va Van Hoa Mien Bac Xa Hoi Chu Nghia Viet Nam 1960–1975* (Hanoi, 1978) pp. 111, 139. (Hanoi: Nha Xuat Ban Khoa Hoc Xa Hoi, 1979) pp. 102–3.
8. Ibid., p. 145.
9. 'Agrarian Differentiation in the Southern Region of Vietnam', *Journal of Contemporary Asia,* vol. 14 (1984) no. 3, p. 287. The estimate is based on shipments of rice out of the Mekong delta plus consumption requirements of urban and non agricultural populations in the delta, taking into account the availability of imported supplies.
10. Tran Huu Quang ('Nhan dien co cau giai cap o nong thon dong bang song Cuu Long', *Nghien Cuu Kinh Te,* no. 128, August 1982, p. 34) says 'The middle peasant is the one who produces about three-quarters of the volume of *commodity* paddy of the delta, i.e. more than one million tonnes.' On the basis of this we can estimate total commodity paddy at about 1.3m tonnes in 1978 (the date of the survey to which the article refers). In 1978 total paddy output of the delta is estimated at 4m tonnes (see Table 4.3) so the share of commodity grain would be about one-third.
11. White, op. cit., p. 101. The cities are apparently excepted from this. In Ho Chi Minh City, I was told that the aim is to achieve rice self-sufficiency for the rural population of the city only, with urban dwellers being supplied by the central government.
12. These include the northern highland and midland provinces of Lang Son, Bac Thai, Vinh Phu and Quang Ninh; the central coastal provinces of Nghe Tinh, Binh Tri Thien and Thuan Hai; and Song Be province in Eastern Nam Bo.
13. *Far Eastern Economic Review,* 28 April 1988, p. 76.
14. *So Lieu Thong Ke 1930–84,* pp. 18–19, 90–1; *So Lieu Thong Ke 1979,* pp. 56–7.
15. *SWB,* FE/W1372/A/36, 15 January 1986; *Far Eastern Economic Review,* 28 April 1988, p. 76.
16. *So Lieu Thong Ke, 1982,* p. 12; *1930–84,* pp. 13–14.
17. In April 1985 it was reported that a feed shortage had caused a decline in

the number of pigs (*SWB*, FE/W1335/A/27, 24 April 1985). It seems likely that this decline occurred in the grain-scarce northern half of the country.

18. Most of these seem to have gone to the more heavily damaged central coastal provinces and highlands (see *SWB*, FE/W858/A/34, 31 December 1975; FE/W873/A/32, 14 April 1976). Thanh Hoa province alone was reported to have sent over 10 000 breeding pigs to the central coastal provinces.

19. In 1975 the North contained three-quarters of the recorded pig population. Given the conditions of the South at that period, as many peasants came to grips with the new economic system for the first time, it is not certain how much reliance can be placed on the 1975 data and some of the improvement may also be due to more accurate records. By 1980 the Northern share had fallen to 65 per cent. *So Lieu Thong Ke 1930–84*, p. 123.

20. 'Collectivisation des terres et crise de l'économie rurale dans le delta du Mekong (1976–80)', *Annales de Géographie*, no. 519, September-October 1984, p. 561.

21. *Vietnam Courier*, no. 8, 1984.

22. *SWB*, FE/W1271/A/23, 25 January 1984; FE/W1275/A/29, 22 February 1984.

23. *SWB*, FE/7729/B/2, 23 August 1984.

24. See Christine White, op. cit. Official procurement prices in the DRV were initially set (in 1954) in such a way that they reflected prevailing free market prices in areas which had been under the control of the independence movement (ibid., p. 102). White points out that the top priority accorded to maintenance of price stability under war conditions in later years meant that changes in costs of production and in supply and demand conditions were not taken into account. This point applies with double force to the attempt to transfer official prices prevailing in the DRV to the South after 1975.

25. Cf. Le Duan's argument, at the Thai Binh agricultural conference in 1974, that the new social relations created by the 'national democratic revolution' and collectivisation had created the pre-conditions for socialist transformation, rather than the latter being the outcome of large-scale industry. In Le Duan and Pham Van Dong, *Towards Large-Scale Socialist Agricultural Production*, (Hanoi: FLPH, 1975) p. 32.

26. See, for example, *SWB*, FE/W838/A/31, 6 August 1975; FE/W869/A/34, 17 March 1976; FE/W874/A/36, 21 April 1976; FE/W875/A/35, 28 April 1976; FE/W881/A/31, 9 June 1976; FE/W896/A/34-35, 22 September 1976.

27. Tran Thanh Phuong, *Minh Hai Dia Chi*, (Ca Mau: Nha Xuat Ban Ca Mau, 1985) pp. 147, 149, 152.

28. Tran Thanh Phuong, *Nhung Trang Ve An Giang*, (Ho Chi Minh City: Van Nghe An Giang, 1984) pp. 121–125; *Cuu Long Thanh Tuu 10 Nam*, (Ho Chi Minh City: Nha Xuat Ban Cuu Long, 1985) pp. 71–73.

29. Nguyen Van Linh, *Thanh Pho Ho Chi Minh 10 Nam* (Hanoi: Su Th.at, 1985) p. 247.

30.   Ibid., p. 106.
31.   Ibid., pp. 108, 168.
32.   Truong Chinh, 'Political Report to the Congress', *SWB*, FE/8447/C1/ 20, 20 December 1986.
33.   Ho Duc Hung, *Cong Nghiep Phuc Vu Nong Nghiep* (Ho Chi Minh City: Nha Xuat Ban Thanh Pho Ho Chi Minh, 1984) pp. 30–1 (my translation).
34.   *SWB*, FE/W1315/A/33, 28 November 1984.
35.   See, for example, *SWB*, FE/W875/A/27, 28 April 1976; FE/W829/A/24, 4 June 1975; FE/W835/A/32, 16 July 1975; FE/W836/A/29–30, 23 July 1975; FE/W845/A/36, 24 September 1975; FE/W848/A/38, 15 October 1975; FE/W849/A/31, 22 October 1975; FE/W853/A/29, 19 November 1975; FE/W858/A/31, 31 December 1975; FE/W859/A/27, 7 January 1976; FE/W861/A/31, 21 January 1976; FE/W864/A/31, 11 February 1976; FE/W/873/A/32, 14 April 1976. Three-quarters of the total fuel supply was allocated to the South according to the then Minister for Material Supply (ibid., p. A/40).
36.   In interviews with Nguyen Huu Tho, Agricultural Editor of *Nhan Dan* and Dao Van Tap, Director of the Vietnamese Social Science Committee (October 1985).
37.   *Far Eastern Economic Review*, 23 July 1987.
38.   IMF, *Direction of Trade Statistics*, 1982, 1987; *So Lieu Thong Ke, 1930– 84*, pp. 120–1.
39.   *Far Eastern Economic Review*, 16 July 1987, p. 57.
40.   IMF, 'Socialist Republic of Vietnam – Recent Economic Developments' (Washington, 1982).
41.   *Far Eastern Economic Review*, 23 July 1987, p. 31.
42.   Barry Wain, *The Refused* (New York: Simon & Schuster 1981); Bruce Grant et al., *The Boat People* (Melbourne: Penguin, 1979).
43.   IMF, 'Vietnam – Staff Report for the 1983 Article IV Consultation', Washington, 13 June 1983.
44.   Adam Fforde, 'Economic Aspects of the Soviet-Vietnamese Relationship' in Robert Cassen (ed.), *Soviet Interests in the Third World* (London: Royal Institute of International Affairs/Sage, 1985).
45.   *Far Eastern Economic Review*, 23 July 1987, p. 29.
46.   Socialist Republic of Vietnam, 'Law on Foreign Investment in Vietnam', mimeo, 29 December 1987.
47.   See, for example, 'Vo Van Kiet's Economic Report', *SWB*, FE/8449/C1/ 6, 23 December 1986.

Bibliography

ARCHIVES

French National Archives: Dépôt des archives d'Outre-Mer, Aix-en-Provence:
    Service Économique.
    Conseiller aux Affaires Économiques (Saigon).
    Fonds des Amiraux.
Declassified Documents Reference System, Carrollton Press, Arlington, Virgi-
    nia, 1975–82.

OTHER SOURCES

An Outline History of the Vietnam Workers' Party, 2nd edn. Hanoi: Foreign
    Languages Publishing House, 1978.
ANDRUS, J. R. 'Preliminary Survey of the Economy of French Indochina',
    US Department of State, June 1943 (mimeo).
Annuaire du Syndicat des Planteurs de Caoutchouc de l'Indochine 1931, Saigon,
    1931.
APPLETON, JUDITH 'Socialist Vietnam: Continuity and Change', in David
    A. M. Lea and D. P. Chaudhri (eds), *Rural Development and the State*,
    London: Methuen, 1983.
ASIAN DEVELOPMENT BANK, *South East Asia's Economy in the 1970s*
    London: Longman, 1971.
BENNETT, JOHN T. 'Political Implications of Economic Change: South
    Vietnam', *Asian Survey*, vol. VII, (1967) no. 8, August.
BERESFORD, M., CATLEY, R. AND PILKINGTON, F. 'America's New
    Pacific Rim Strategy', *Journal of Contemporary Asia*, vol. 9 (1979), no. 1.
BERESFORD, MELANIE 'Agriculture in the Transition to Socialism: the
    Case of South Vietnam', in Mats Lundahl (ed.), *The Primary Sector in
    Economic Development*, London: Croom Helm, 1985.
BERESFORD, MELANIE 'Vietnam: Northernizing the South or Southerniz-
    ing the North', *Contemporary Southeast Asia*, vol. 8, (1987) no. 3.
BERNARD, PAUL *Le Problème Économique Indochinois*, Paris: Nouvelles
    Éditions Latines, 1934.
BERNARD, PAUL *Nouveaux Aspects du Problème Économique Indochinois*,
    Paris: Fernand Sorlot, 1937.
BHADURI, AMIT *Agricultural Co-operatives in North Vietnam*, ILO, Rural
    Employment Policy Research Programme, Working Paper WEP 10/WP/6,
    Geneva, March 1976.
BIDELEUX, ROBERT *Communism and Development*, London and New
    York: Methuen, 1985.
BRUGGER, BILL (ed.) *Marxism in Flux*, London and Sydney: Croom Helm,
    1985.
BURCHETT, WILFRED *My Visit to the Liberated Zones of South Vietnam*,
    Hanoi: Foreign Languages Publishing House, 1966.

BURR, J. M. 'Land-To-The-Tiller: Land Redistribution in South Vietnam 1970–1973', PhD thesis, University of Oregon, 1976.

BUSINESS INTERNATIONAL ASIA/PACIFIC LTD *Risks and Rewards in Vietnam's Markets: Business Approaches to North and South Vietnam*, Hong Kong, 1974.

BUSZYNSKI, L. *Soviet Foreign Policy and Southeast Asia*, London: Croom Helm, 1986.

BUTTINGER, JOSEPH *Vietnam: A Dragon Embattled*, 2 vols. New York: Praeger, 1967.

CALLISON, C. STUART 'The Land-To-The-Tiller Program and Rural Resource Mobilisation in the Mekong Delta of South Vietnam', *Papers in International Studies, Southeast Asia Series*, no. 34, Ohio University, 1974.

CARTON, P. *Le Caoutchouc en Indochine*, Hanoi, 1924.

CASELLA, ALEXANDER 'Dateline Vietnam: Managing the Peace', *Foreign Policy*, (1978) no. 30, Spring.

CATLEY, R. AND McFARLANE, B. 'The Vietnamese Social Model', *Australian Quarterly*, vol. 46, (1974) no. 4, December.

CHALIAND, GERARD *The Peasants of North Vietnam*, Harmondsworth: Penguin, 1969.

CHAMBRE DE COMMERCE DU PORT DE HAIPHONG *Statistiques Commerciales*, (Haiphong: IDEO, 1936, 1937.)

CHAMBRE DE COMMERCE DE SAIGON, *Situation Commerciale*, Saigon: Imprimerie Nouvelle Albert Portail, 1924.

CHESNEAUX, JEAN, *The Vietnamese Nation: Contribution to a History* (tr. M. Salmon), Sydney: Current Book Distributors, 1966.

CHI DO PHAM 'Inflationary Finance in Wartime South Vietnam, 1960–1972', PhD thesis, University of Pennsylvania, 1976.

CHILD, F. C., *Essays on Economic Growth, Capital Formation and Public Policy in Vietnam*, Saigon: Michigan State University Vietnam Advisory Group, 1961.

CITIBANK *Vietnam: An Economic Study*, Hong Kong, 1976.

CLARK, D. L. 'Planning and the Real Origins of Input-Output Analysis', *Journal of Contemporary Asia*, vol. 14 (1984) no. 4.

COMITÉ ÉCONOMIQUE, Session des 5, 6 et 7 Mai 1947, Dalat, *Compte-Rendu Analytique et Procés-verbaux*, supplement au *Bulletin de Renseignements Économiques*, Juin 1947.

Communist Party of Viet Nam *4th National Congress Documents*, Hanoi: FLPH, 1977.

Constitution of the Socialist Republic of Vietnam, Hanoi: FLPH, 1981.

Cuu Long Thanh Tuu 10 Nam (Cuu Long: 10 Years' Success), Ho Chi Minh City: Nha Xuat Ban Cuu Long, 1985.

DANH SON 'Raw Materials in the Effort to Build and Perfect the Production Structure in Our Country', *Nghien Cuu Kinh Te*, no. 6, November-December 1981, translated in JPRS 80671, *Vietnam Report*, no. 2361.

DAO XUAN SAM 'A Proper Approach to the Application of the Transitional Economic Forms and Management System', *Viet Nam Social Sciences*, no. 1, 1985.

DEPUY, OCTAVE *Étude Comparative sur la Culture de l'*Hevea Brasiliensis *en Cochinchine et dans les divers pays du Moyen-Orient*, Paris, 1912.

DESCOURS-GATIN C. AND VILLIERS H. *Guide de Recherches sur le Vietnam,* Paris: L'Harmattan, 1983.

DE SILVA, S. B. D. *The Political Economy of Underdevelopment,* London: Routledge & Kegan Paul, 1982.

DOBB, MAURICE *On Economic Theory and Socialism,* London: Routledge & Kegan Paul, 1955.

DOBB, MAURICE *An Essay on Economic Growth and Planning,* London: Routledge & Kegan Paul, 1960.

DOBB MAURICE *Papers on Capitalism, Development and Planning,* London: Routledge & Kegan Paul, 1967.

DOMAR, EVSEY *Essays in the Theory of Economic Growth* (New York: Oxford University Press, 1957).

DOAN MINH QUAN AND J-P POLINIÈRE *Future of Natural Rubber in Vietnam,* mimeo, 1970.

DRV *The Democratic Republic of Vietnam,* Hanoi: FLPH, 1975.

DUIKER, WILLIAM *Vietnam Since the Fall of Saigon,* Athens, Ohio: Ohio University Centre for International Studies, 1980.

Economic Restoration and Cultural Development in the Democratic Republic of Vietnam (1955–1957), Hanoi: FLPH, 1958.

ECONOMIST INTELLIGENCE UNIT, *Quarterly Economic Review: Indochina,* 1971, 1972.

ELLIOTT, DAVID W. P. 'Revolutionary Re-integration: A Comparison of the Foundation of Post-Liberation Political Systems in North Vietnam and China', PhD thesis, Cornell University, 1976.

ELLMAN, M. *Socialist Planning,* Cambridge University Press, 1979.

FALL, BERNARD *The Two Vietnams: A Political and Military Analysis,* London: Pall Mall Press, 1963.

FAR EASTERN ECONOMIC REVIEW *Asia Yearbook 1982,* Hong Kong, 1982.

FÉDÉRATION INDOCHINOISE *Bulletin de Renseignements Économiques,* No. 12, 15 July 1947.

FFORDE, ADAM, *Problems of Agricultural Development in North Vietnam,* PhD thesis, University of Cambridge, 1982.

FFORDE, ADAM 'Economic Aspects of the Soviet-Vietnamese Relationship' in Robert Cassen (ed.), *Soviet Interests in the Third World,* London: Royal Institute of International Affairs/Sage, 1985.

FFORDE, ADAM AND PAINE, SUZANNE H. *The Limits of National Liberation,* London: Croom Helm, 1987.

FRASER, STEWART E. 'Vietnam's Population: Current Notes', *Contemporary Southeast Asia,* vol. 6 (1984) no. 1, June.

GENERAL STATISTICAL OFFICE *Tinh Hinh Phat Trien Kinh Te va Van Hoa Mien Bac Xa Hoi Chu Nghia Viet Nam 1960–75* (Economic and Cultural Development of Socialist North Vietnam 1960–75), Hanoi, 1978.

GENERAL STATISTICAL OFFICE *30 Nam Phat Trien Kinh Te va Van Hoa Cua Nuoc Viet Nam Dan Chu Cong Hoa* (30 Years' Economic and Cultural Development of the DRV), Hanoi: Su That, 1978.

GENERAL STATISTICAL OFFICE *So Lieu Thong Ke 1978* (Statistical Data of the Socialist Republic of Vietnam), Hanoi, 1979.

GENERAL STATISTICAL OFFICE *So Lieu Thong Ke 1979,* Hanoi, 1980.

GENERAL STATISTICAL OFFICE *So Lieu Thong Ke 1982*, Hanoi, 1983.

GENERAL STATISTICAL OFFICE *So Lieu Thong Ke 1930–1984*, Hanoi: Nha Xuat Ban Thong Ke, 1985.

GHAI, D., KHAN, A. R., LEE, E. AND RADWAN, S. *Agrarian Systems and Rural Development*, London: Macmillan, 1979.

GONZALES, NANCY 'The Organisation of Work in China's Communes', *Science*, vol. 217 (1982) no. 4563, 3 September.

GORDON, ALEC 'North Vietnam's Collectivisation Campaigns', *Journal of Contemporary Asia*, vol. 11 (1981) no. 1.

GORDON, ALEC 'Notes on "Subsistence" Agriculture and the Transition to Socialism in Vietnam', mimeo, University of Bielefeld (n.d.).

GOUROU, PIERRE *L'Utilisation du Sol en Indochine Français*, Paris: Hartmann, 1940.

GOUROU, PIERRE *Les Paysans du Delta Tonkinois*, Paris: Mouton, 1965.

GOUVERNEMENT GÉNÉRAL DE L'INDOCHINE *Annuaire Statistique de l'Indochine*, 1913 à 1922, 1923 à 1929, 1930–31, 1931–32, 1932–33, 1934–35–36, 1936–37, 1941–42, Hanoi: IDEO; 1943–46, Saigon: Statistique Général de l'Indochine, 1948.

GOUVERNEMENT GÉNÉRAL DE L'INDOCHINE *Budget General: Compte Administratif, Exercice 1937*, Hanoi: IDEO, 1938.

GOUVERNEMENT GÉNÉRAL DE L'INDOCHINE *Chemins de Fer: Statistiques* Hanoi-Haiphong: IDEO.

GOUVERNEMENT GÉNÉRAL DE L'INDOCHINE Direction des Affaires économiques, *Annuaire économique de l'Indochine 1926–27*, Hanoi: IDEO, 1927.

GOUVERNEMENT GÉNÉRAL DE L'INDOCHINE *Rapports au Grand Conseil des Intérêts Économiques et Financiers et au Conseil de Gouvernement*, Hanoi: IDEO, 1929, 1930, 1936; Hanoi: Imprimerie G. Taupin & Cie, 1938.

GOUVERNEMENT GÉNÉRAL DE L'INDOCHINE *Rapport sur la Navigation et le Mouvement Commercial de l'Indochine pendant l'année 1922*, Hanoi-Haiphong: IDEO, 1928.

GOUVERNEMENT GÉNÉRAL DE L'INDOCHINE *Supplément statistique mensuel au Bulletin économique de l'Indochine*, January 1939, January 1940.

GRANT, BRUCE *The Boat People*, Melbourne: Penguin, 1979.

HAMILTON, CLIVE 'Capitalist Industrialisation in the "Four Little Tigers" of East Asia' in P. Limqueco and B. McFarlane (eds), *Neo-Marxist Theories of Development*, London: Croom Helm, 1983.

HILL, R. D. 'Aspects of Land Development in Vietnam' *Contemporary Southeast Asia*, vol. 5 (1984) no. 4, March.

HINTON, WILLIAM 'A Trip to Fengyang County', *Monthly Review*, November 1983.

HINTON, WILLIAM 'More on China's New Family Contract System', *Monthly Review*, April 1984.

HO DUC HUNG *Cong Nghiep Phuc Vu Nong Nghiep* (Industry Serving Agriculture) Ho Chi Minh City: Nha Xuat Ban Thanh Pho Ho Chi Minh, 1984.

HOANG ANH 'Pricing Activities in the New Situation', *Tap Chi Cong San*, no. 6, June 1978, translated in JPRS 71773, *Translations on Vietnam* no. 2057.

HOANG DUC NGHI 'Making Rational and Economic Use of Material Resources in the National Economy', *Tap Chi Hoat Dong Khoa Hoc* (Scientific Review), no. 7, July 1982, translated in JPRS 82098, *Vietnam Report,* no. 2405.

HODGKIN, T. *Vietnam: The Revolutionary Path,* London: Macmillan, 1981.

HOLLOS, MARIDA 'The Effects of Collectivisation on Village Social Organisation in Hungary', *East European Quarterly,* vol. XVII (1983) no. 1, March.

HONEY, P. J. (ed.) *North Vietnam Today: Profile of a Communist Satellite,* New York: Praeger, 1962.

HOUTART, FRANÇOIS AND LEMERCINIER, GENEVIÈVE *Sociologie d'une Commune Vietnamienne,* CRSR, Louvain-la-Neuve: Université Catholique de Louvain, 1981.

HUMPHREY, C. *Karl Marx Collective* Cambridge and Paris: Cambridge University Press and Éditions de la Maison des Sciences de l'Homme, 1983.

HUYNH KIM KHANH *Vietnamese Communism 1925–1945,* Ithaca and London: Cornell University Press, 1982.

IBRD 'Current Economic Position and Prospects of the Republic of Vietnam', Report no. 315-VN, 18 January 1974.

IMF 'Socialist Republic of Vietnam – Recent Economic Developments', 18 May 1982.

IMF 'Vietnam – Staff Report for the 1983 Article IV Consultation', June 1983.

INDUSTRIAL DEVELOPMENT BANK OF VIETNAM *Industrial Development News,* Saigon.

ISHIKAWA, S. *Essays on Technology, Employment and Institutions in Development: Comparative Asian Experience,* Tokyo: Kikokuniya, 1981.

JACOBS, BRUCE J. 'Political and Economic Organisational Changes and Continuities in Six Chinese Rural Localities', *Australian Journal of Chinese Affairs,* no. 14, July 1985.

JASNY, NAUM *Soviet Economists of the Twenties: Names to be Remembered,* Cambridge University Press, 1972.

JONES, GAVIN W. 'Population Trends and Policies in Vietnam', *Population and Development Review,* vol. 8, (1982) no. 4, December.

KALECKI, MICHAL *Selected Essays on the Economic Growth of the Socialist and Mixed Economy,* Cambridge University Press, 1972.

KASER, M. C. (ed.) *Economic Development for Eastern Europe,* London and New York: Macmillan and St. Martins Press, 1968.

KASER, M. C. AND PORTES, R. (eds) *Planning and Market Relations,* London and New York: Macmillan and St. Martins Press, 1971.

KEITH, RONALD C. (ed.) *Energy Security and Economic Development in East Asia,* London and Sydney: Croom Helm, 1986.

KERR, PRUE 'Adam Smith on Growth – Again', paper presented to the Third Conference of the History of Economic Thought Society of Australia, Melbourne, May 17–20 1985.

KIM NGOC 'Determined to Correct the Shortcomings and Steadily Advance the Co-operativisation Movement and Agricultural Production in Vinh Phu Province', *Hoc Tap,* no. 6, June 1969, translated in JPRS, *Translations on North Vietnam,* no. 583.

KOLKO, GABRIEL, *The Roots of American Foreign Policy,* Boston: Beacon Press, 1969.

KOLKO, GABRIEL *Vietnam: Anatomy of a War 1940–1975*, London and Sydney: Allen & Unwin, 1986.

KORNAI, JANOS *Growth, Shortage and Efficiency: A Macrodynamic Model of the Socialist Economy*, Oxford: Blackwell, 1982.

KUZNETS, S. 'International Differences in Capital Formation and Financing' in Universities-National Bureau Committee of Economic Research, *Capital Formation and Economic Growth: A Conference*, Princeton University Press, 1955.

KYN, O 'The Role of Prices in a Socialist Economy' in M. Kaser (ed.) *Economic Development for Eastern Europe*, London: Macmillan, 1968.

LAM THANH LIEM 'Collectivisation des Terres et Crise de l'Économie rurale dans le Delta du Mekong (1976–1980)', *Annales de Géographie*, no. 519, 1984.

LAM THANH LIEM 'Nouvelles Reforms et Crise persistante de l'Économie rurale dans le Delta du Mekong de 1981 à 1985', *Annales de Géographie*, (1985) no. 524, July-August.

LE CHAU *Le Viet Nam socialiste: une économie de transition*, Paris: Maspero, 1966.

LE DUAN AND PHAM VAN DONG *Towards Large-Scale Socialist Agricultural Production*, Hanoi: FLPH, 1975.

LE DUAN *The Vietnamese Revolution: Fundamental Problems, Essential Tasks*, Hanoi: FLPH, 1978.

LE DUAN *Vietnam: Social and Economic Problems of the '80s*, Hanoi: FLPH, 1984.

LE DUAN 'Get a Good Hold of the Laws and Renovate Economic Management', *Viet Nam Social Sciences*, No. 2, 1984.

LE DUC THO 'Improve Agricultural Management', *Southeast Asia Chronicle*, no. 93, April 1984.

LE KHOA *et al. Tinh Hinh Kinh Te Mien Nam 1955–1975* (Economic Situation in Southern Vietnam 1955–1975), Ho Chi Minh City: Social Science Commission, 1979.

LE NHAT QUANG 'Mechanisation of Crop Growing in the Mekong River Delta', *Nghien Cuu Kinh Te*, 1975, translated in JPRS 76711, *Vietnam Report*, no. 2222.

LE THANH KHOI *Socialisme et Développement au Vietnam*, Paris: Presses Universitaires de France, 1978.

LE THU Y 'Improve Planning in Agricultural Co-operatives', *Nghien Cuu Kinh Te*, no. 87, September-October 1975, translated in JPRS 66638, *Translations on Vietnam* no. 1759.

LE VINH 'Grasp the Line of the Party and Advance to Building Large-Scale Socialist Production in Our Country', *Nghien Cuu Kinh Te*, 1977, translated in JPRS 69071, *Translations on Vietnam*.

LELE, D. Y. 'Report to the Government of the Republic of Vietnam on the Improvement of Agricultural Statistics', Rome: FAO, 1967.

LENIN, V. I. 'New Data on the Laws Governing the Development of Capitalism in Agriculture' [1915], *Collected Works*, vol. 22, Moscow: Progress Publishers, 1964.

LENIN, V. I. 'The Agrarian Question and the Critics of Marx' [1901], *Collected Works*, vol. 5, Moscow: Progress Publishers, 1973.

LENIN, V. I. *The Development of Capitalism in Russia,* Moscow: FLPH, 1956.

LIMQUECO, P. AND McFARLANE, B. 'Problems of Economic Planning for Underdeveloped Socialist Countries', *Journal of Contemporary Asia,* vol. 9 (1979). no. 1.

LIU GUOGUANG 'Aspects and Problems of Price Reform in China', mimeo, Centre for Asian Studies, University of Adelaide, March 1986.

LOWE, ADOLF 'Structural Analysis of Real Capital Formation', Universities-National Bureau Committee of Economic Research, *Capital Formation and Economic Growth: A Conference,* Princeton University Press, 1955.

MACKINTOSH, MAUREEN, 'Agricultural Price Policies in Support of Agrarian Transformation in Centrally Planned Economics in Africa', mimeo, paper prepared for the workshop on 'Transformation of the agrarian system in centrally planned economies in Africa', Arusha: FAO, October 1983.

MACLEAR, MICHAEL *Vietnam: The Ten Thousand Day War,* London: Thames Methuen, 1981.

MARR, DAVID 'Central Vietnam Rebuilds: An Eyewitness Account', *Indochina Issues,* no. 59, July 1985.

MARX, KARL *Capital,* Vol. I, Moscow: Progress Publishers, n.d.

McFARLANE, BRUCE, 'Political Economy of Class Struggle and Economic Growth in China 1950-1982', *World Development,* vol. 11 (1983) no. 8.

McFARLANE, BRUCE 'Political Crisis and East European Economic Reforms', in Paul G. Lewis, *Eastern Europe: Political Crisis and Legitimation,* London and Sydney: Croom Helm, 1984.

McFARLANE, BRUCE *Yugoslavia: Politics, Economics and Society,* London: Frances Pinter, 1988.

MINISTRY OF FINANCE *Nhung Van De Chu Yeu Trong Phap Lenh Thue Nong Nghiep* (Principal Problems of the Agricultural Tax Law) Hanoi: Nha Xua Ban Su That, 1985.

MOISE, E. E. 'Land Reform and Land Reform Errors', *Pacific Affairs,* vol. 49, 1976.

MONTIAS, J. M. 'Price Setting Problems in the Polish Economy', *Journal of Political Economy,* vol. LXV (1957) no. 6, December.

MOODY, DALE L. 'The Manufacturing Sector in the Republic of Vietnam', PhD thesis, University of Florida, 1975.

MORROW, MICHAEL 'Vietnam's Embargoed Economy: in the US Interest?', *Indochina Issues,* no. 3, August 1979.

MURRAY, MARTIN J. *The Development of Capitalism in Colonial Indochina (1870–1940),* Berkeley: University of California Press, 1980.

MUSOLF, LLOYD D. 'Public Enterprise and Development Perspectives in South Vietnam', *Asian Survey,* vol. III (1963) no. 8, August.

NATIONAL BANK OF VIETNAM *Annual Report,* Saigon, 1968.

NATIONAL BANK OF VIETNAM *Economic Bulletin,* Saigon (some issues in French as *Bulletin Économique*).

NATIONAL INSTITUTE OF STATISTICS *Economic Situation in Vietnam,* Ministry of Planning and National Development, Saigon (some issues in Vietnamese only as *Tinh Hinh Kinh Te Viet Nam*).

NATIONAL INSTITUTE OF STATISTICS *Monthly Bulletin of Statistics,* Saigon.

NATIONAL INSTITUTE OF STATISTICS *Statistical Yearbook*, Saigon.

NG SHUI MENG 'Vietnam in 1983: Keeping a Delicate Balance', *Southeast Asian Affairs*, 1984.

NGO VINH LONG *Before the Revolution*, Cambridge, Mass.: MIT Press, 1973.

NGO VINH LONG 'Agrarian Differentiation in the Southern Region of Vietnam', *Journal of Contemporary Asia*, vol. 14 (1984) no. 3.

NGUYEN DUC NHUAN 'Les Contradictions de l'Organisation Scientifique de l'Espace et du Travail agricoles au Nord-Vietnam', *L'Espace géographique*, vol. XI (1982) no. 2.

NGUYEN HUU DONG 'Agriculture collective, Agriculture familiale, Économie socialiste: quelques Hypothèses', *Vietnam*, no. 1, December 1980.

NGUYEN KHAC VIEN *Southern Vietnam (1975–1985)*, Hanoi: FLPH, 1985.

NGUYEN KIEN *Le Sud-Vietnam Depuis Dien Bien Phu*, Paris: Maspero, 1963.

NGUYEN TIEN HUNG, G. *Economic Development of Socialist Vietnam, 1955–1980*, New York: Praeger, 1977.

NGUYEN VAN LINH *Thanh Pho Ho Chi Minh 10 Nam* (Ho Chi Minh City: 10 Years), Hanoi: Su That, 1985.

NGUYEN XUAN LAI 'The Family Economy of Co-operative Farmers', *Vietnamese Studies*, no. 13, (n.d.).

NOLAN, PETER 'De-Collectivisation of Agriculture in China 1979–82: A Long Term Perspective', *Economic and Political Weekly*, 6 August 1983.

NOLAN, PETER 'From Collective Farms to Co-operatives', *China Now*, no. 108, Spring 1984.

NORLUND, IRENE 'Rice Production in Colonial Vietnam 1900–1930', in Irene Norlund, Sven Cederroth and Ingela Gerdin (eds), *Rice Societies: Asian Problems and Prospects*, London and Riverdale: Curzon/Riverdale, 1986.

NORLUND, IRENE 'The Role of Industry in Vietnam's Development Strategy', *Journal of Contemporary Asia*, vol. 14 (1984) no. 1.

NYLAND, CHRIS 'Vietnam, the Plan/Market Contradiction and the Transition to Socialism', *Journal of Contemporary Asia*, vol. 11 (1981) no. 4.

On the Eve of the 6th Congress of the Communist Party of Vietnam 1976–86, Hanoi: FLPH, 1986.

PARTI COMMUNISTE DU VIETNAM *Ve Congrès National: Rapport Politique* (Hanoi: Editions en Langues étrangères, 1982).

Pentagon Papers (as published by the *New York Times*), London: Routledge & Kegan Paul, 1971.

PHAM CUONG AND NGUYEN VAN BA *Revolution in the Village: Nam Hong (1945–1975)*, Hanoi: FLPH, 1976.

PHAN LE PHUONG 'Several Thoughts Concerning the Application of Market Relations in Planning', *So Tay Giang Vien*, 1977, translated in JPRS 70675, *Translations on Vietnam*, no. 2013.

POPKIN, SAMUEL L. *The Rational Peasant*, Berkeley: University of California Press, 1979.

PORTER, GARETH 'Imperialism and Social Structure in Twentieth Century Vietnam', PhD thesis, Cornell University, 1976.

PORTER, GARETH, Vietnam's Long Road to Socialism', *Current History*, vol. 71, 1976.

PREOBRAZHENSKY, E. A. *The Crisis of Soviet Industrialisation: Selected Essays*, (Donald A. Filtzer, ed.), London: Macmillan, 1980.

Programme et Budget de l'Office Indochinois du Riz, Archives de l'Office Indochinois du Riz, no. 6, 1936, no. 12, 1939.

RACE, JEFFREY, *War Comes to Long An*, Berkeley: University of California Press, 1972.

Rapport annuel de l'Institut des Recherches sur le Caoutchouc au Vietnam, Saigon.

RAWSKI, THOMAS, *China's Transition to Industrialism*, Ann Arbor: University of Michigan Press, 1980.

REGLAR, STEVE 'The Law of Value Debate – A Tribute to the Late Sun Yefang' in Bill Brugger (ed.) *Marxism in Flux 1978–84*, London and Sydney: Croom Helm, 1985.

ROBEQUAIN, CHARLES *The Economic Development of French Indochina*, New York: Oxford University Press, 1944.

SACHS, IGNACY AND KASIMIERZ LASKI 'Industrial Development Strategy' *Industrialisation and Productivity*, Bulletin 16, New York: United Nations, 1971.

SANSOM, ROBERT L. *The Economics of Insurgency in the Mekong Delta of Vietnam*, Cambridge, Mass. and London: MIT Press, 1970.

SCIGLIANO, ROBERT *Vietnam: Nation Under Stress*, Boston: Houghton Mifflin, 1964.

SEN, ABHIJIT 'Market Failure and Control of Labour Power: Towards an Explanation of "Structure" and Change in Indian Agriculture' Parts I and II, *Cambridge Journal of Economics*, vol. 5 (1981) nos. 3 and 4.

SIAMWALLA, A. AND HAYKIN, S. *The World Rice Market: Structure, Conduct and Performance*, International Food Policy Research Institute, Research Report no. 39, June 1983.

SMITH, ADAM *Wealth of Nations* (Cannan edn), London: Methuen, 1961.

SNEPP, FRANK *Decent Interval*, New York: Random House, 1977.

Southeast Asia Chronicle, special issue on Vietnam, no. 76, December 1980.

SPOOR, MAX 'Finance in a Socialist Transition: the Case of the Democratic Republic of Vietnam (1955–1964)', *Journal of Contemporary Asia*, vol. 17 (1987) no. 3.

SPULBER, N. (ed.) *Foundations of Soviet Strategy for Economic Growth*, Bloomington: University of Indiana Press, 1964.

STANFORD RESEARCH INSTITUTE *Land Reform in Vietnam*, Menlo Park, California, 1968.

STATISTIQUE GÉNÉRALE DE L'INDOCHINE *L'Évolution de l'Économie indochinoise*, 1947, 1948, 1949, Supplément au *Bulletin Économique de l'Indochine*, Saigon.

STOLLERU, LIONEL G. 'An Optimal Policy for Economic Growth', *Econometrica*, vol. 33 (1965) no. 2, April.

TAYLOR, MILTON C. 'South Vietnam: Lavish Aid, Limited Progress', *Pacific Affairs*, vol. XXXIV, (1961) no. 3, Fall.

THOMPSON, VIRGINIA *French Indo-China*, London: George Allen and Unwin, 1937.

THRIFT, NIGEL AND FORBES, DEAN *The Price of War: Urbanization in Vietnam 1954–1985,* London: Allen & Unwin, 1986.

TON THAT TIEN 'Vietnam's New Economic Policy: Notes and Comments', *Pacific Affairs,* vol. 56, 1983.

TRAN HUU QUANG 'Nhan dien co cau giai cap o nong thon dong bang song Cuu Long' (Identifying class structure in the rural areas of the Mekong delta), *Nghien Cuu Kinh Te,* no. 128, 1982.

TRAN THANH PHUONG *Minh Hai Dia Chi* (Geography of Minh Hai), Ca Mau: Nha Xuat Ban Mui Ca Mau, 1985.

TRAN THANH PHUONG *Nhung Trang Ve An Giang* (Pages on An Giang), Ho Chi Minh City: Van Nghe An Giang, 1984.

TRINH XUAN TIEN 'The Present State of the Grain Market', *Tap Chi Cong San,* no. 11, November 1979, translated in JPRS 74929, *Vietnam Report,* no. 2163.

TRUED, M. N. 'South Vietnam's Industrial Development Centre', *Pacific Affairs,* vol. 33, 1960.

TRULLINGER, JAMES W. *Village at War,* New York and London: Longman, 1980.

TRUONG CHINH 'Political Report to the Congress', BBC, *SWB,* FE/8447, 20 December 1986.

TSAI MAW KUEY *Les Chinois au Sud Vietnam,* Paris: Bibliothèque Nationale, 1968.

US DEPARTMENT OF AGRICULTURE *Agricultural Statistics,* Washington DC: US Government Printing Office.

US DEPARTMENT OF COMMERCE *Report on Indochina Rubber Industry and Siamese Rubber Production Outlook,* Washington DC: US Government Printing Office, 1946.

VICKERMAN, ANDREW 'A Note on the Role of Industry in Vietnam's Development Strategy', *Journal of Contemporary Asia,* vol. 15 (1985) no. 2.

VIEN SU HOC *Nong Dan Viet Nam Tien Len Chu Nghia Xa Hoi,* (Vietnamese Peasants Advance Towards Socialism), Nha Xuat Ban Khoa Hoc Xa Hoi, Hanoi, 1979.

VIETNAM COUNCIL ON FOREIGN RELATIONS *Vietnam Economic Report,* Saigon.

Vietnam Documents and Research Notes, Saigon: USAID Mission in Vietnam.

Vietnamese Studies, Special Issue on Agricultural Problems, no. 51, Hanoi. (n.d.).

Vietnamese Studies, 'Economic Policy and National Liberation War', no. 44, Hanoi, 1976.

VO NHAN TRI *Croissance économique de la République démocratique du Vietnam,* Hanoi: Éditions en langues étrangères, 1967.

VO VAN KIET *Thuc Hien Dong Bo 3 Cuoc Cach Mang o Nong Thon* (Carrying Out the 3 Revolutions in the Countryside), Ho Chi Minh City: Nha Xuat Ban Thanh Pho Ho Chi Minh, 1985.

WADEKIN, KARL-EUGEN *The Private Sector in Soviet Agriculture,* Berkeley: University of California Press, 1973.

WAIN, BARRY, *The Refused: The Agony of the Indo-China Refugees,* New York: Simon & Schuster, 1981.

WATSON, A. 'Agriculture Looks for "Shoes that Fit": The Production

Responsibility System and its Implications', in N. Maxwell and B. McFarlane (eds) *China's Changed Road to Development*, Oxford: Pergamon Press, 1984.

WERNER, JAYNE 'Socialist Development: The Political Economy of Agrarian Reform in Vietnam', *Bulletin of Concerned Asian Scholars*, vol. 16 (1984) no. 2.

WHITE, CHRISTINE P. 'Debates in Vietnamese Development Policy', IDS, *Discussion Paper*, no. 171, March 1982.

WHITE, CHRISTINE 'Socialist Transformation of Agriculture and Gender Relations: the Vietnamese Case', IDS, *Bulletin*, vol. 13 (1982) no. 4, September.

WHITE, CHRISTINE 'Reforming Relations of Production: Family and Co-operative in Vietnamese Agricultural Policy', mimeo, Institute of Development Studies, University of Sussex, (n.d.).

WHITE, CHRISTINE, 'Agricultural Planning, Pricing Policy and Cooperatives in Vietnam' *World Development*, vol. 13 (1985) no. 1.

WHITE, GORDON 'Political Economy of Vietnamisation', *Eastern Horizon*, vol. 11 (1972) no. 2.

WIEDEMANN, PAUL 'The Origins and Development of Agro-Industrial Development in Bulgaria' in R. A. Francisco, B. A. Laird and R. D. Laird (eds), *Agricultural Policies in the USSR and Eastern Europe*, Boulder: Westview Press, 1980.

WIEGERSMA, NANCY 'Agrarian Differentiation in the Southern Region of Vietnam: A Comment', *Journal of Contemporary Asia*, vol. 15 (1985) no. 4.

WILEY, PETER 'Vietnam and the Pacific Rim Strategy', *Leviathan*, vol. 1 (1969) no. 3, June.

WOODSIDE, ALEXANDER *Community and Revolution in Vietnam*, Boston: Houghton Mifflin, 1976.

WORLD BANK 'The Socialist Republic of Vietnam, An Introductory Report', report no. 1718-VN, 12 August 1977.

XU DIXIN *China's Search for Economic Growth*, Beijing: New World Press, 1982.

XUE MUQIAO *China's Socialist Economy*, Beijing: Foreign Languages Press, 1981.

NEWSPAPERS AND PERIODICALS

Far Eastern Economic Review, Hong Kong.
Financial Times, London.
IMF, *Direction of Trade Statistics*, Washington.
IMF, *International Financial Statistics*, Washington.
JPRS, *Translations on Vietnam*, Washington.
JPRS, *Vietnam Report*, Washington.
JPRS, *Southeast Asia Report*, Washington.
SIPRI Yearbook, Stockholm.
Summary of World Broadcasts: Far East, BBC, London.
The Far East and Australasia, London.
Vietnam Courier, Hanoi.
World Bank, *World Development Report*, New York.

Index

Agriculture   12, 63–5, Chs 4 & 5 *passim*, 164, 195–7, 231–2
  and self–sufficiency   142, 147–8, 223
  and VCP policy   90–3, 96–8, 114, 146, 175, 275
  collectivisation of   3, 12–13, 92, 100, 102–5, 107, 109–21, 127–9, Ch. 5 *passim*, 143, 180, 191, 206, 219, 226, 263, 267
  cycles in   131–3, 137
  development strategies towards   48, 54, 86, 90–3, 113–14, 140, 177, 191–6
  employment in   65, 76–8
  fertiliser in   82, 93, 102, 107, 122–4, 126, 134, 151, 211, 225, 231, 261
  in NLF areas   95–7, 101–3, 217
  incentives in   13, 109, 117, 127, 132, 136, 139, 143–53, 156, 159–60, 171, 232, 269
  large scale   103, 114, 129, 131, 139–43, 152, 267
  livestock production in   107–8, 225–6, 277–8
  markets in   13, 131–2, 136, 219–20
  mechanisation of   78, 101–2, 112, 122–4, 134, 140, 152–3, 155, 158, 261, 265–6, 269
  output of sector   13, 66, 69–70, 86, 92–3, 112, 114, 118, 122, 137–8, 142, 180–1, 183–4, 211, 222, 224–6, 232, 234, 255, 263
  prices   117, 126, 148–9, 198, 268, 278
  procurement by State   113–15, 117–19, 126, 130, 147–9, 183, 218–22, 226, 255, 263, 268, 278
  product contract system in   107, 117, 127, 135–6, 157–8, 198, 215, 224, 226, 265
  productivity in   13, 50, 93, 95, 100, 102, 107, 111–12, 123, 130, 136–7, 139, 143, 145, 152, 154–5, 164–5, 170, 175, 240, 266–7, 269
  relations with industry   92, 98–9, 128, 140, 147, 152, 161, 176–84, 195, 229–34
  sharecropping in   9, 151–2, 156
  specialisation in   105, 107, 140, 142, 219, 231, 235, 241
  State farms   103, 105–8, 134, 262, 275
  (*see also* Cooperatives; Investment; Production Collectives)

Aid   72–3, 75, 79, 87–8, 91, 134, 172–5, 187, 197–8, 235, 272, 274
  American 1, 4, 6, 12, 48, 53–8, 62, 65, 71–2, 74, 79–82, 85, 92, 98, 102, 129, 134, 162, 174, 216, 220, 228, 240, 253–4
  Chinese   7, 46, 88, 91, 134, 148, 165, 173, 175, 184, 197, 240, 265, 273
  composition of   173–4, 197, 257
  reduction of   6, 12, 72, 74, 85, 130, 134, 148, 162, 175, 184, 197, 216, 220, 228, 240–1, 253, 257, 265
  Soviet   46, 88, 91, 134, 165, 173, 197–8, 236, 275
  Swedish   198, 202
An Giang province   102, 117, 124, 218, 263
Annam   8, 16–20, 23, 25–44, 246
Army, expenditure on   275
Artisan industries   3, 18, 57, 99, 124, 164–6, 168, 188, 197, 200, 209, 216, 223, 229, 268, 274
Asian Development Bank   65, 75
Autarky   7, 9–11, 14, 17–18, 99, 111, 114, 128, 130, 142, 147–8, 164, 169, 175, 205, 208, 211, 215, 217–18, 223, 228, 235, 240, 242

Balance of payments   54–5, 66, 79, 80, 257
Ben Tre province   120, 122, 124, 256
Bernard, Paul   22, 26, 163–4, 245
Binh Tri Thien province   259, 277
Black market   76–7, 146–7, 210, 216, 220–1, 227, 237
'Boat people' (escapees)   6, 77, 182
Bombing (by USA)   4, 13, 25, 66, 134, 146, 164, 166–8, 172, 201
Budgets   149, 174, 210
  deficits   207, 210
  of DRV   174
  of French colonialists   11, 21–7, 45, 245
  of RVN   54, 56, 80, 252
Bukharin, N. I.   170, 176–80, 188, 244, 273
Bureaucracy   15, 52, 92, 131, 161, 179–80, 197, 203–4, 208, 212, 242, 271

Cambodian conflict   92, 106, 114

Capacity utilisation 126, 146, 149, 181–2, 196, 201, 207, 210
Capital formation 55, 58–60, 62–3, 84, 187, 251 (*see also* Investment)
Capital-output ratio 14, 54, 58–9, 73, 85–6, 88, 91, 145
Capital, trading 22, 27, 65, 114
Chemical industry 168, 197, 231, 274–5
China 1, 177, 201–2, 239, 244
  agrarian experience of 13, 74, 130–3, 136, 139–40, 142, 144–7, 153–4, 180, 265–6, 270
  conflict with 5–6, 92, 116, 146, 184, 187, 201, 217, 235
  trade with Vietnam 18, 24, 134, 265 (*see also* Aid; Economic reform)
Chinese ethnic group (Hoa) 22, 27, 51–2, 83, 114, 116, 184, 250, 273
Cholon 20, 27, 31, 114
Circulation of capital 213–14
  of goods 3, 8, 27–37, 78, 128–9, 205, 207, 213–15, 241, 260
Climate 110, 132, 148, 185, 227, 234, 239
Coal 19, 28, 30, 75, 116, 172, 181, 197, 205, 274
Cochin-China 8, 11, 16–46, 164, 246
Colonialism 9, 12
  French 11, 17, 19–20, 24, 26
Commercial Import Program 56, 62, 69, 81–2, 252
Commodity production 9, 14, 78–9, 99, 111, 128, 131, 177, Ch. 7 *passim*, 240, 242–3
Competition (*see* Market forces)
Consumption 23, 48, 55, 58, 80, 84–8, 95, 137, 144–7, 155–6, 170–2, 175, 197–8, 210, 212, 233 (*see also* Living standards)
Cooperatives 104, 106, 109, 121, 123–8, 132–3, 136–8, 144, 147, 153, 155–6, 158, 160, 208, 219
  distribution in 126, 132–3, 137–8, 143–4, 149–52, 155, 167, 266, 270
  industrial 124, 229, 231
  investment in 120–1, 144, 161
  labour mobilisation in 74, 93, 102, 124, 126, 130, 137–9, 149, 154, 156, 159, 240
  nominal 135, 138, 142
  production in 121, 132
  successful 121–2, 127, 138, 220
Corruption, under Thieu regime 57, 62, 257

in SRV 114, 205, 209, 221, 242
Corvée labour 38, 75
Council for Mutual Economic Assistance (CMEA) 7, 88, 197–8, 236–8
Credit 125, 207, 253–4, 264
Currency reform 119, 210–11, 276
Cuu Long province 102, 121, 199, 263

Debt, external 12, 235–6, 257
Decentralisation 128, 131–3, 204–8, 215, 232, 241–2
Democratic Republic of Vietnam (DRV) 19, 45–6, 91, 96
  economy of 6, 46, 88, 91, 130, 163–8, 172–5, 217–18, 224, 228
Disproportionalities 13, 146, 171, 175–87, 191, 202, 215, 218 (*see also* Shortages)
Division of labour 4, 10–14, 76, 79, 86, 99, 111, 121, 129, 139–43, 151, 160, 162, 213–18, 227–8, 231–3, 235, 238, 241–2
  international 6–7, 14, 162, 216, 228, 235, 237–8
Dong Nai province 106–7, 122, 229
Dong Thap province 120

Economic complementarity 4, 6–7, 11, 14, 16, 45, 86, 162, 168, 218, 234–5, 244
Economic growth 5, 8, 50, 53, 55, 58, 60, 62–3, 78, 85–7, 90, 145, 164, 170, 174, 177–9, 186, 188, 191, 197–8, 201, 203, 213, 232, 243, 272
  crisis of 7, 9, 62, 112–13, 117, 129, 179, 183–4, 202, 241
  regional pattern of 9–10, 14, 45, 98, 211, 218–33
  sectoral 7, 14, 59, 63–76, 134–5, 145, 167–8, 175, 188, 191, 195, 235, 251, 254
Economic reform 7, 13, 15, 109, 117–29, 180, 196, 203–12, 214, 215–16, 227, 232–3, 235–6, 241, 276–7
  agrarian 13, 117–29, 131–3, 135–6, 153, 198
  industrial 14, 203–12
  in China 7, 13, 136, 146, 163, 180, 237
  in Hungary 7, 180
  in USSR 7, 163, 238
  (*see also* China, Agrarian experience)
Economic surplus 8–12, 14, 45, 48, 87, 90, 128, 150, 160, 169, 177–8, 213–15, 217, 241–3

in agriculture 5, 12–13, 51, 53, 58, 69, 88, 90, 95, 101, 111, 114, 116–17, 121, 128, 130, 136, 144, 148, 155–7, 222, 224, 234

in collectives 121, 128, 130, 137, 139, 143, 156–9

marketed in agriculture 74, 88, 112–15, 130, 160–1, 169–71, 175, 177–9, 183–4, 211, 215–16, 219–21, 224, 226, 232–3, 240, 277

Economies of scale 6, 13–14, 140, 143, 152, 160, 171, 201, 208, 228, 241–2

Employment 65, 76–8, 85–6, 124, 208, 230–1, 257 (*see also* Agriculture; Manufacturing)

Energy 72, 75, 92, 196–7, 207, 231–2, 275

shortage 108, 181, 211, 237

Exports 6–7, 16–17, 19–21, 24, 28, 44–6, 70, 87, 124, 126, 172, 197–8, 229–32, 234–5

in development strategy 12, 86, 92, 105, 170–2, 177, 191, 237–8, 275

of RVN 52–3, 66, 74, 79, 255

Fforde, A. 137–8, 265, 272, 279

Fishing industry 68, 70, 84, 181–2, 237, 255

Five-Year Plans 215

First (1961–65) 166, 201

Second (1976–80) 3, 14, 86–8, 91, 186, 191–5, 197, 201–2, 265

Third (1981–85) 92, 192–4, 275

Fourth (1986–90) 92, 192–4, 201, 222, 238

Food deficit 16, 69, 222, 224, 229, 241, 277–8

Foodgrains 19, 28, 32, 53, 66–7, 69, 112–15, 117, 122, 137, 147–8, 173, 182–3, 198, 218–22, 263 (*see also* Rice)

Foreign direct investment 54, 59, 70, 82–3, 88, 237, 258

laws governing 6, 237–8, 279

Gourou, Pierre 17, 27, 245, 248

Haiphong 17, 19, 25, 27–9, 33, 209, 246

Handicraft (*see* Artisan industry)

Hanoi 17, 19, 27, 122

Hau Giang province 119

Heavy industry 5, 13–14, 87–8, 90–2, 146, 163, 167–75, 177–81, 191, 195–8, 201, 211, 217, 228–9, 231–3, 235, 241

Ho Chi Minh City 105–6, 114, 122, 181–3, 198–9, 207, 223, 225–6, 230–4, 241, 262, 277

Households 13, 119, 127, 131–2, 139, 153–61, 217, 269–71

relations with collective 131–2, 139, 153–61, 220, 265, 269–70

Imports 18, 53–4, 65, 79, 80, 87, 90, 98, 116, 174, 198, 235

of capital goods 81, 90, 174, 198, 257

of consumer goods 48, 57, 80, 130, 134, 137, 148, 173–4, 198, 205, 228, 240

of inputs 66, 71, 74, 81, 126, 146, 198, 228, 234, 255, 257–8

Incentives 13–14, 85, 117, 175, 200, 203, 205, 209, 212, 215–16, 238, 241–2 (*see also* Agriculture)

Industrialisation 2, 4–6, 14, 51, 55, 57, 59, 91, 129, 140, 143, 150, Ch. 6 *passim*, 227, 235, 243

Industry (*see* Manufacturing)

Inflation 54, 56, 60, 62–3, 65, 80, 121, 146, 150, 207, 211, 237, 241, 253

Investment 6, 52, 55, 58–61, 63, 85–6, 89, 92, 134, 145–7, 150, 170, 172, 174–5, 178–9, 196–8, 202, 211, 215–16, 241, 272

composition of 54–5, 59, 63, 65, 134, 147, 150, 172, 175, 180–1, 195–8, 212, 214, 232–3, 251

effectiveness of 87, 145–7, 171–2, 196–8, 200, 203, 214, 238

in agriculture 66, 79, 93, 128, 137, 144–5, 195, 197, 261, 267 (*see also* Capital formation; Foreign investment)

Irrigation schemes 24, 74–5, 93–4, 103–4, 111, 122–3, 137, 140–2, 266

Kalecki, M. 145, 171, 175, 202, 258, 267, 272

Kien Giang province 119, 182, 231, 261

Korea 1, 12, 49, 50, 55, 57, 59–60, 82–3, 103, 162, 236, 239, 249

Kornai, J. 178, 201, 273

Labour accumulation projects 103, 111–12, 140, 142, 145, 175, 240, 266

Labour control 151–3, 160, 171, 267–9

Labour-intensive techniques 41, 74–5, 124, 126, 141–3, 151–3, 156, 160, 267

Labour market 21, 40

Labour process 9–10, 76, 141–3, 209
Labour productivity 13, 59, 77, 85–6, 107, 112, 122–4, 130, 134, 136–40, 143, 145, 148–50, 152–3, 158, 160–1, 164–5, 170–1, 173, 175, 182–3, 200, 204, 209–10, 217, 235, 266
Lacouture, Jean 16, 244
Land–labour ratios 18, 22, 38, 44, 78, 93, 97, 137
Land reform 12, 47, 51, 58, 60, 66, 82, 95, 100, 103, 122, 217, 250, 255, 259, 263
Land-to-the-Tiller programme 54, 99, 250, 261
Land tenure 49, 93, 99–101, 103, 217, 261
Lang Son province 18, 274, 277
Law of value 131, 153, 214
Le Duan 129, 159, 191, 200–1, 244, 267, 274
Lenin, V. I. 131, 139–41, 153, 159, 179, 227, 267
Living standards 54, 57, 86, 106–9, 132, 144–5, 170, 178, 180, 195, 209, 212, 222, 233, 235, 240 (*see also* Consumption)
Long An province 50, 108–9, 122, 226
Lowe, Adolph 145, 267, 273

Manufacturing 6, 52, 63–5, 216, 223, 228–32, 241, 253, 255–6, 258
  as share of GDP 65, 70
  employment in 77–8, 230–1
  output of 70–3, 198–200
  ownership of 52, 83–4, 250, 258
Mao Zedong 11, 133, 140, 177
Market, and division of labour 10, 171–2, 213–17, 238
  national 9, 13–14, 27, 74, 128, 130, 148, 161, 204–5, 214, 218, 233–8, 241
Market forces 14, 109, 112, 128, 178, 189, 204–5, 208, 213–14, 238, 242
Marx, Karl 4–5, 8, 10, 141, 145, 159, 175–7, 213–14, 268–70
Mekong River delta 12, 16–17, 20, 33, 65–6, 74, 88, 91, 93–6, 98–100, 102–5, 109–13, 115–17, 119–20, 129, 137, 216, 220, 224, 226–7, 229–33, 240–1, 259, 261–2, 270, 277
Minh Hai province 98, 229
Mining 19, 24, 163, 274 (*see also* Coal)
Mode of production 9, 10, 14, 21, 153, 159–60, 213

Nam Bo region 94, 111, 115, 121, 216, 232
National Liberation Front (NLF) 4, 12, 47, 51, 53, 55, 58, 61–3, 65, 74, 94–100, 122, 217, 240, 252–3
New Economic Zones 45, 105–9, 262, 275
Ngo Dinh Diem regime 48–54, 57, 69, 78, 93, 248–9
Ngo Vinh Long 42, 104, 220, 259–60, 263
Nguyen Huu Dong 154, 265, 269–70
Nguyen Tien Hung, G. 16, 32, 173, 244–5, 272
Nolan, Peter 144, 147
North Vietnam (*see* Democratic Republic of Vietnam)

Oil exploration 75–6, 187, 198, 274

Paine, Suzanne 244, 265, 272
Paris Peace Talks/Agreement 62, 66, 93, 96, 167, 274
Peasantry 41–2, 62, 69, 72, 94–5, 97, 99–101, 103–5, 109–12, 119, 122, 128, 132, 135–6, 138, 142, 161, 169–71, 173, 175–80, 231, 240
Phoenix Program 78, 96, 112
Phu Khanh province 105
Planning, economic 14, 128, 178–9, 185–91, 202–7, 211–12, 214–16, 221, 232, 239–40, 242, 273
Plantation workers 33, 35, 37–45, 107, 247
Police methods, French 42–3
Political cycle 179, 191
Population ix, 23–4, 58–60, 130, 137, 148, 170–1, 212, 224–5, 252
  density of 21, 38, 41, 104, 111, 115, 247, 259, 261–2
  movement of 45, 248, 251–2, 262
Preobrazhensky, E. 179, 267, 273
Price stabilisation 65, 115, 117, 210–11, 278
Producer-goods industries 90–1, 145, 147, 165, 169–70, 172, 174, 176, 191, 195–8, 201–2, 211, 234, 272–3
Production collectives 75, 109–10, 119, 121–2, 124, 133
Production, organisation of 8, 86, 119, 146, 209, 213
Public works 21, 23–6, 33, 38, 41
  of Thieu regime 257
  (*see also* Labour accumulation projects)

Quang Nam Da Nang province 224, 260

Rawski, T. 201–2, 275
Red River delta 17, 27–8, 38, 143, 224, 259, 261
Republic of Vietnam 11, 47–89, 224
Rice 22, 28, 30, 32–3, 35, 41, 46, 53, 55, 62, 65–6, 69, 93–5, 98, 112–13, 115, 173, 183, 219, 246
exports 16, 20–1, 24, 66, 74, 79, 95, 251, 254
imports 68, 130, 134, 148, 254–5, 265
Robequain, C. 18, 245–6
Rubber 20, 22, 33–4, 38–41, 45, 55, 66, 68, 87, 97–8, 105–7, 198, 237, 247, 254
exports 20–1, 44, 66, 79, 251

Saigon 17, 20, 25, 27–8, 31, 63, 76, 98 (*see also* Ho Chi Minh City)
Self-sufficiency in grain 16, 19, 46, 91, 93, 117, 130, 134
Sen, Abhijit 151–2, 267
Shortages 5, 6, 12, 14, 72, 74–7, 87, 101–2, 108, 114, 116, 124, 126, 130, 146–7, 149, 154, 158, 175–6, 178, 181–5, 202, 208–11, 216, 220, 227, 229, 232–3, 237, 241–2, 264, 277–8
of foreign exchange 6, 87, 116, 128, 170, 228
Smith, Adam 10, 214
Socialism (*see* cooperatives; Karl Marx; Vietnamese Communist Party; V. I. Lenin; Social relations)
Social relations 8, 9, 11, 47, 49–60, 78, 99, 111, 119, 131, 140, 156–7, 162, 191, 242–3, 250, 265–6
capitalist 3, 8, 9, 49, 99–100, 111, 128, 216, 243, 263, 270
socialist 8, 119, 127–8, 139–40, 191, 206, 242–3, 267, 270
Song Be province 105, 107–8, 122, 223, 277
Soviet Union agrarian experiences 131, 153–4, 269–70
exports to 198
imports from 198
industrialisation debate 163, 168, 176–80, 244
Vietnam relations with 236, 239
Spare parts 87, 124, 178, 181–2, 202, 228
Specialisation 10, 18, 217–18, 238, 242 (*see also* Agriculture)

Steel 201–2
Stolleru, L. G. 258, 272
Subsistence 10, 86, 95, 138, 145, 149, 154, 156, 161, 173, 208–9, 219, 222, 234, 270

Taiwan 1, 13, 49–50, 57, 59–60, 82, 103, 162, 239, 258
Taxation 56, 216, 260
colonial 20–2
in NLF zones 97–8, 260
of agriculture 69, 114, 117, 126, 137, 144, 158, 174, 219, 264
Tay Ninh province 75, 105–6, 182, 205, 218
Technology 8, 13, 134, 140–2, 146, 152, 177, 191, 201–2, 209, 214, 231, 241, 269
Tet Offensive 54–5, 61–3, 96, 99
Textiles 19, 28, 30–1, 57, 70–1, 92, 172, 230, 253
Thai Nguyen 201, 274
Thanh Hoa province 18, 28, 278
Thieu regime 8, 48, 54–5, 69, 78, 82, 85, 94, 99, 112, 132, 228–9, 244, 252–3
Thompson, Virginia 42, 246
Three Year Plan (1958–60) 92, 272
Thuan Hai province 105, 277
Tien Giang province 261
Tonkin 8, 16, 19, 20, 23, 25–43, 163, 246
Trade between areas of Vietnam 16, 18–19, 21, 27–46, 162–3, 204–5, 207, 228, 233–5, 241, 271, 279
in humans 33, 34, 38–45, 246
international 6, 7, 20, 24–5, 27, 54, 65, 126, 170–2, 198, 205–6, 231–2, 235–6, 238
Transport 5, 18, 20, 74, 98, 124, 148, 172, 234, 241
air 74
rail 18, 23–5, 33–5, 38, 75, 172, 181, 246–7, 256
road 20, 24, 35–6, 74, 241, 247, 256
shipping 18, 27–33, 74, 223, 246
water 18, 20, 24, 28, 74, 241
Trung Bo region 110, 240, 259, 261
Truong Chinh 3, 245, 263, 274

Unemployment 76–8, 208, 276
Unification ix, 1–15, 23, 90, 218
and growth 168, 238
economic ix, 4, 7, 8, 11, 23, 48, 65, 113, 162, 217, 233–43
political 16, 234, 239

United States 1, 12, 248
  blockade of Vietnam 5, 82, 87, 184,
    236, 256, 274
  (*see also* Aid; Bombing)

Viet Minh 25, 49–50, 54, 95, 99
Vietnamese Communist Party (VCP) 3,
  10–11, 16, 95, 206, 208, 260
  Congresses of 3, 4, 92, 166, 191, 197,
    205–8
  strategies of 3, 13, 51, 93, 109, 114,
    117, 163, 191–5, 206, 210
Vinh Phu province 202, 277
Vo Van Kiet 127, 202–4, 212, 275

Wadekin, K-E. 154–5, 269
Wage labour 41, 151–2, 156, 231
Wages 53, 56–7, 76–7, 86, 107, 156,
  183, 208–10, 222, 269
War, effects of 4, 5, 7, 13, 55–6, 60, 66,
  73–4, 76, 79, 93, 105–6, 111, 134,
  146, 166–8, 172, 184, 201, 233, 238–
  41, 259, 264
White, Christine 155, 219, 259, 265,
  268, 270, 277
Women's work 76–7, 155, 265

Yugoslavia 9, 242

NATIONAL UNIFICATION AND ECONOMIC DEVELOPMENT IN VIETNAM